Donna Kooler's
Kool Felt Embroidery

Donna Kooler's
Kool Felt Embroidery

Donna Kooler with Linda Gillum

LARK BOOKS

A Division of Sterling Publishing Co., Inc.

New York / London

Senior Editor
Ray Hemachandra

Editor
Larry Shea

Art Director
Stacey Budge

Assistant Editor
Mark Bloom

Illustrators
Bernie Wolf
Orrin Lundgren

Photographer
Stewart O'Shields

Cover Designer
Susan McBride

Library of Congress Cataloging-in-Publication Data

Kooler, Donna.
  [Embroidered felt projects]
  Donna Kooler's kool felt embroidery / Donna Kooler with Linda Gillum
-- 1st ed.
    p. cm.
  Includes index.
  ISBN 978-1-60059-250-8 (pb-trade pbk. : alk. paper)
  1. Embroidery--Patterns. 2. Felt work. I. Kooler, Donna. II. Title.
  TT770.K57 2009
  746.44'041--dc22
                              2008025570

10 9 8 7 6 5 4 3 2 1

First Edition

Published by Lark Books, A Division of
Sterling Publishing Co., Inc.
387 Park Avenue South, New York, NY 10016

Text © 2009, Donna Kooler and Linda Gillum
Photography © 2009, Lark Books unless otherwise specified
Illustrations © 2009, Lark Books unless otherwise specified

Distributed in Canada by Sterling Publishing,
c/o Canadian Manda Group, 165 Dufferin Street
Toronto, Ontario, Canada M6K 3H6

Distributed in the United Kingdom by GMC Distribution Services,
Castle Place, 166 High Street, Lewes, East Sussex, England BN7 1XU

Distributed in Australia by Capricorn Link (Australia) Pty Ltd.,
P.O. Box 704, Windsor, NSW 2756 Australia

If you have questions or comments about this book, please contact:
Lark Books
67 Broadway
Asheville, NC 28801
828-253-0467

Manufactured in China

ISBN 13: 978-1-60059-250-8

For information about custom editions, special sales, and premium and corporate purchases, please
contact the Sterling Special Sales Department at 800-805-5489 or specialsales@sterlingpub.com.

Contents

The Projects

Bright Morning Pillow 22

Barrel Candy Bracelet 25

Twirling Flower Coasters 27

Spiral Illusion Electronics Carrier 29

I ♥ Books Bookmark 32

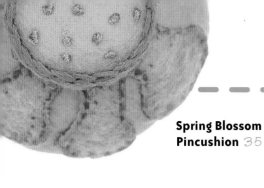

Spring Blossom Pincushion 35

Pretty Kitty Appliqué 37

Rainbow Band Bracelet 39

Flower Power Hobo Bag 73

Book Buddy Blossom 44

Fun & Funky Appliqués 46

Green Garden Headrest 50

Heartwarming Electronics Holster 55

Fairy Tale Fantasy Pincushion 53

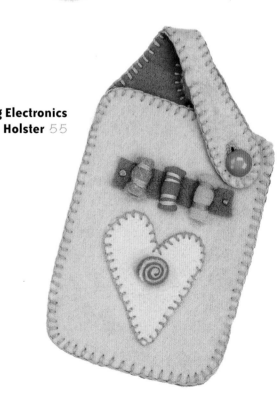

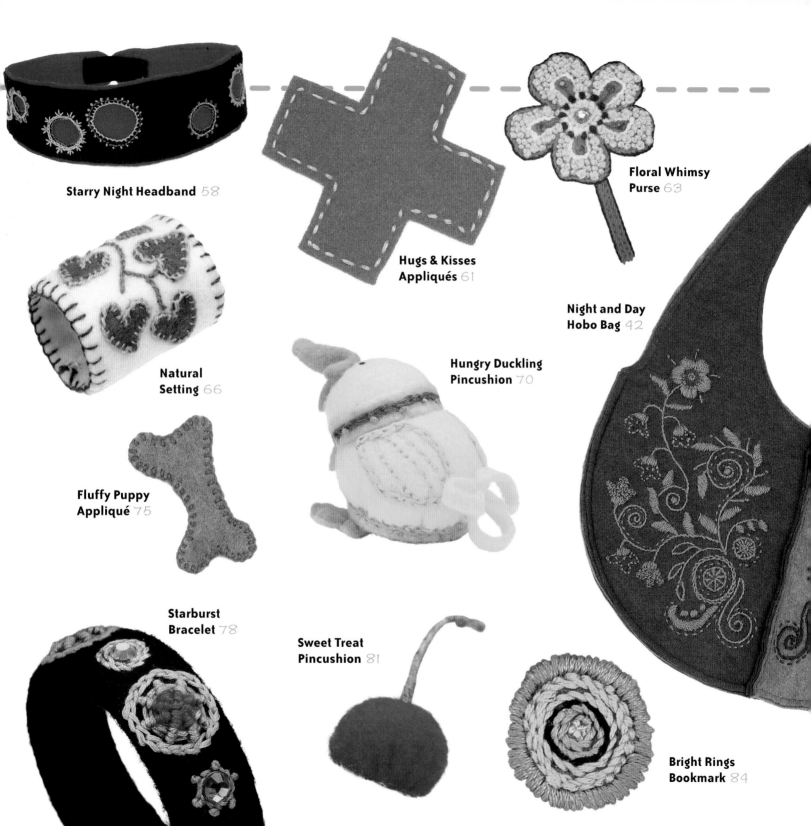

Starry Night Headband 58

Hugs & Kisses Appliqués 61

Floral Whimsy Purse 63

Natural Setting 66

Night and Day Hobo Bag 42

Hungry Duckling Pincushion 70

Fluffy Puppy Appliqué 75

Starburst Bracelet 78

Sweet Treat Pincushion 81

Bright Rings Bookmark 84

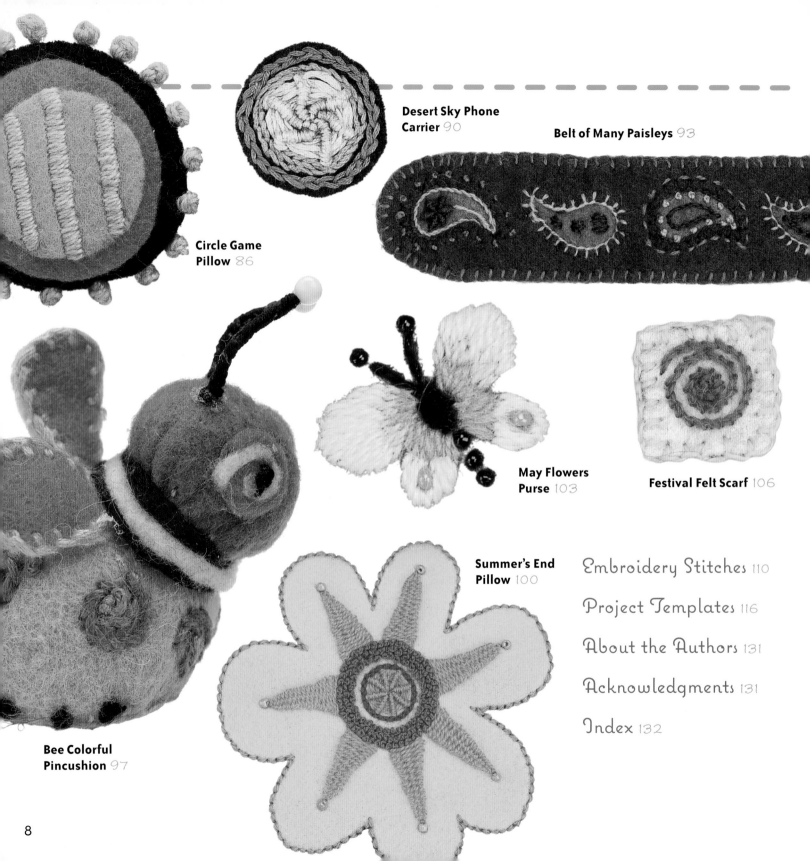

Introduction

Felted fabric is versatile, useful, and great fun to work with. You can cut it, shape it, and poke it with needles, as well as paint it, glue it, and stitch it. The bold colors of this smooth surface perfectly complement embroidery work, allowing the yarn, floss, or thread to really pop.

In this book we present fresh designs for home and fashion accessories—items like pillows, pincushions, appliqués, and much more. What makes these projects especially interesting are the embellishments, such as wonderful small felt patches you embroider in exquisite detail, and the beads, sequins, and other fun flourishes you can add. The beautiful projects we've selected emphasize individual creativity. Let your imagination run wild. Making simple changes in color or personalizing the embellishments will transform these projects into your own unique creations.

In the Basics section, you'll learn about all the materials and techniques you need to make the finished designs. You'll learn how to cut the felt in the provided patterns, layer the pieces in complementary colors, and embroider them with fanciful swirls, beautiful borders, and decorative stitches. Embroidery and felt go together

so well because felt has no grain: It's easy to embroider intricate designs in any shape, without worrying about how the fabric will react.

The projects will inspire you to experiment, and with so many possibilities, you'll never lack for ideas. Want a pincushion that's as useful as it is appealing? Turn to embroidered felt, and projects like the Spring Blossom Pincushion (page 35). Need a purse that will stand up to pencil points or keys? Again, embroidered felt is ideal (see page 63). Looking for a tough but tiny carrier for your cell phone or essential tunes? Embroidered felt is the answer (see pages 29, 55, and 90). Scarves are traditional felt projects, but the great scarf included here (page 106) is unlike any you've seen before, with multiple colors, layers, and pom-poms.

Every day is a very good day to indulge in making this wonderful traditional art and craft with modern flair. So select a project, pick up a needle, and discover that wherever you go around the wide world, felt, embroidery, and your own creative fancy go together beautifully.

Donna Kooler
Linda Gillum

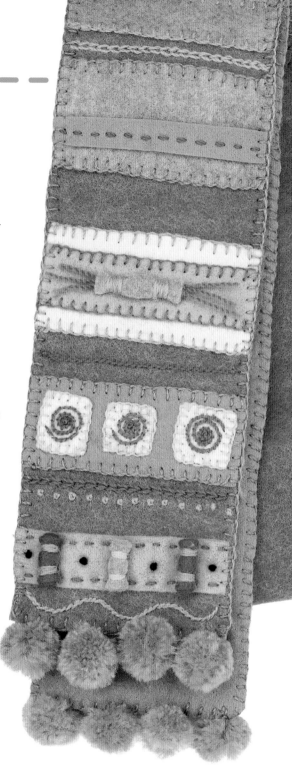

Basics

Materials

To complete the projects in this book, you'll need supplies. First and foremost on the list is felt fabric, but on the following pages, you'll find descriptions of all the basic materials and supplies.

Felt Fabric

Felt is made from loose webs of natural or synthetic fibers that are locked together by the combination of moisture, heat, and repeated pressure to create a wonderful fabric for clothing as well as art and craft projects. With no raw edges, felt doesn't ravel, which makes it ideal for many craft projects. You can use three types of felt for the projects in this book: wool felt, wool/rayon felt, and synthetic felt.

Wool felt is made from natural fibers. Available in many colors, it has a beautiful look and feel. You can purchase it locally or online as cut pieces or as yardage. Yardage widths vary, so note the width before you buy. Wool/rayon blend felt resembles 100 percent wool felt, but is less expensive because of the addition of rayon fibers. Projects made with wool or wool/rayon felt should be dry-cleaned.

Synthetic felt is made from 100 percent acrylic fibers and comes in many colors. Very reasonably priced, it is available in local craft and fabric stores as well as online. Like the other types of felt, you can buy it as cut pieces or as yardage, usually 72 inches (182.9 cm) wide. While you can hand- and machine-wash it, you should lay it flat to dry.

Other Materials

You'll need just a few other things to make the wonderful creations in this book, although most of these materials are probably in your house already, especially if you enjoy creative hand-work. If you don't have some of the supplies on the list, a quick trip to your neighborhood craft store will solve the problem.

Wool embroidery yarn
  (e.g., Paternayan yarn)

Embroidery floss
  (e.g., DMC floss)

Measuring tape or ruler

Pencil

Freezer paper

Tracing paper

Straight pins

Large sewing scissors

Small embroidery scissors

Water-erasable marking pen

Sewing thread in colors
  to match your felt

Sewing and tapestry needles

Nap riser brush

Polyester fiberfill

Rotary cutter, clear ruler,
  and cutting mat (optional)

Sewing machine (optional)

Fabric glue

Basic Techniques

Got your supplies on hand? You'll also need to know some basic (as in simple and easy-to-learn) techniques to make the projects you'll find in this book. The following sections begin with general techniques for cutting felt and working with patterns, and then move on to step-by-step instructions for constructing bags, pillows, purses, felt swirls, and more.

Using a Rotary Cutter

Cut straight lines through fabrics quickly and easily with a rotary cutter, a self-healing mat, and a clear plastic ruler. Often, these tools are sold as a set. Review the instructions included in the package. Here are a few things to remember when working with a rotary cutter:

* The blade is very sharp, so be sure to engage the safety guard when the cutter is not in use, even if you lay it down for just a minute! Also, keep the cutter out of the reach of children and pets.

* Make sure the blade is sharp and free of fabric bits. If the cutter isn't working properly, check that the nut holding the blade is not too tight or too loose.

* Lay your fabric on the self-healing mat and line up the clear ruler with the lines on the mat. Press firmly on the ruler with your non-dominant hand, taking care that your fingers are not too close to the cutting edge.

Hold the rotary cutter with your dominant hand and stand so that your head is directly over the blade and you can see the cutting line. Position the blade next to the ruler, but lean the top slightly away from the ruler. Always cut away from your body by pressing and rolling the blade along the edge of the ruler. Peel away the cut fabric and continue with your next cut.

* You can stack fabric layers to cut multiple pieces at one time, but make sure the layers are not too thick or the cutter might bunch the fabric or cut inaccurately.

Making Pattern Pieces

You can choose from a variety of ways to make pattern pieces:

* If you're making a simple shape, trace the pattern onto tracing paper. Pin the tracing paper onto the felt and cut out the shape. Leave the pattern pinned to the felt until you're ready to use it.

* Freezer paper also makes easy-to-use pattern pieces. Trace the shape onto the smooth side of the freezer paper and cut loosely around the tracing. Place the shiny or waxy side of the paper on the felt and press it lightly with an iron. The freezer paper will stick to the felt and make the shape easy to cut.

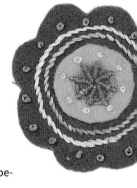

* For patterns with embroidery designs, transfer the pattern and the embroidery design at the same time, using the transfer method described below.

Transferring Designs

Trace the design onto tracing paper. Poke small holes in the paper about $1/8$ inch (3 mm) apart along the design lines. Gently dab inside each hole with a water-erasable marking pen to leave a mark through the tracing paper onto the felt. Remove the tracing paper and if the design is hard to read, connect the dots with the marking pen.

Constructing a Basic Pillow

1 After completing the embroidery on the pillow top, pin the top and bottom, with right sides together. Sew the front to the back using the recommended seam allowance and a thread that matches the color of the pillow top. Leave a 5-inch (12.7 cm) opening for turning along the bottom edge. If you are stitching by hand, use a backstitch.

2 Turn the pillow right side out. Stuff it with polyester fiberfill to the desired fullness. Pin and hand-stitch the opening closed.

Constructing a Hobo Bag

1 Cut out four pieces of one color felt and four pieces of a contrasting color, using the pattern on page 130.

2 Complete any decorative stitching before constructing the bag.

3 Place two pieces of the same color felt together. Top stitch the curved edges together, 1/4 inch (6 mm) from the edge. Repeat three more times to make four purse quarters. Make sure the embroidered pieces are on top to make the bag front.

4 Place the contrasting purse quarters together, right sides facing out. Stitch them together using a 1/4-inch (6 mm) seam along the bottom curve only, stopping the seam 1/4 inch (6 mm) from the center edge (figure 1).

5 Stitch each pair of the purse straps together (wrong sides together at the top of the straps) using 1/4-inch (6 mm) seams (figure 2). Make the seams on the outside (the right side).

6 Place the purse halves together and stitch the two fronts together using a 1/4-inch (6 mm) seam (figure 3). Repeat to join the two back sections. Like the straps, these seams are also on the outside of the purse.

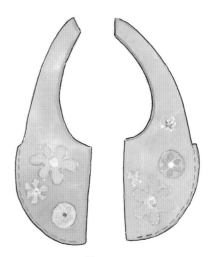

Figure 1

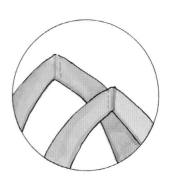

Figure 2

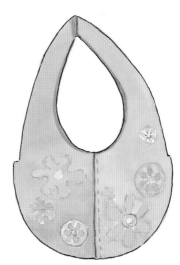

Figure 3

Constructing a Purse

1 Cut one strap of each color to 60 x 1½ inches (152.4 x 3.8 cm). Sew the end of each strap together using a ¼-inch (6 mm) seam to form a complete circle.

2 Place the straps wrong sides together, matching the seams. Pin them in place (figure 4).

3 Stitch the edges together using a ¼-inch (6 mm) seam.

4 Pin the embellished front onto the contrasting piece of felt. Sew along the top using a ½-inch (1.3 cm) seam. Repeat for the back piece.

5 Position the seam on the strap at the center of the purse's bottom edge (figure 5). Pin the strap to the purse front piece.

6 Stitch the purse front to the strap using a ¼-inch (6 mm) seam (figure 6). Then pin the strap to the purse back piece.

7 Stitch the purse back to the strap using a ¼-inch (6 mm) seam (figure 7).

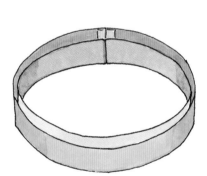

Figure 4

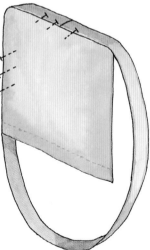

Figure 5

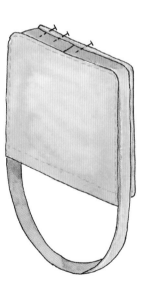

Figure 6

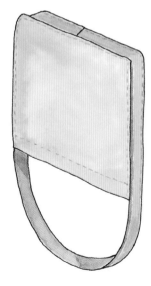

Figure 7

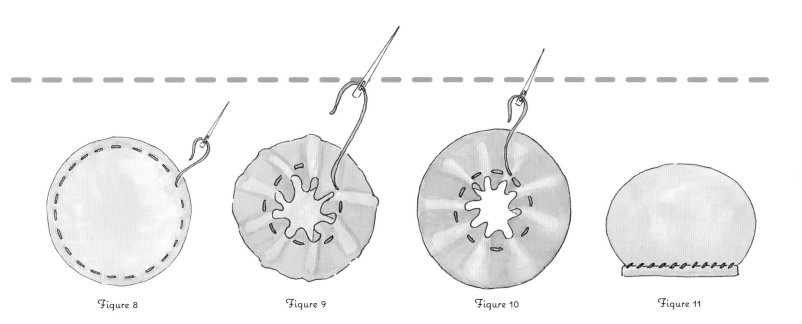

Figure 8   Figure 9   Figure 10   Figure 11

Constructing a Pincushion

1 Cut out a small circle of lightweight cardboard to the desired dimensions for the pincushion base.

2 Cut the first felt circle to the correct diameter (approximately twice as large as the cardboard base). Sew a running stitch around the perimeter of this felt piece, $\frac{1}{8}$ inch (3 mm) from the outside edge. Leave the thread on the needle (figure 8).

3 Place the cardboard base in the middle of the felt and gently pull the thread to gather and stretch the felt firmly around the cardboard (figure 9). Smooth the felt and stretch it slightly to fit. Knot the thread to secure the stitches.

4 Cut out another felt circle to size for the body piece. Sew a running stitch around the perimeter of the body piece, $\frac{1}{8}$ inch (3 mm) from the outside edge (figure 8 again). Leave the

thread on the needle and pull it gently to gather and edges and form the body. Fill the body with small bits of fiberfill until you have the shape and firmness you want (figure 10). Pull the thread to further shape the body. Knot the thread.

5 Apply a small amount of glue to the bottom of the pincushion and place it in the center of the base with the stitched side up. Let the glue dry. Secure the pincushion in place using a whipstitch (figure 11).

6 If you are adding another shape to the pincushion, repeat step 4 to create and stuff the new piece. Press it onto the body at the appropriate spot, pin or glue it in place, and then stitch the pieces together with a whipstitch.

Making a Felt Swirl

1 Cut two pieces of contrasting felt to the same desired size.

2 Lightly apply fabric glue to the outside piece of felt and place the contrasting piece ¼ inch (6 mm) below the top edge.

3 Trim the bottom ends so they align.

4 Firmly roll up the swirl (figure 12). Glue the end down, making sure the outer color covers the inner color. Trim the end of the inner color if necessary.

5 Allow the glue to dry and trim the swirl with sharp scissors, if necessary, for desired size.

Figure 12

Making a Felt Bead

1 Cut a rectangle of felt to the desired size. Cut a second rectangle ⅜ inch (1 cm) shorter.

2 Machine-stitch the larger rectangle with decorative vertical stitches, beginning about ⅓ inch (8.5 mm) from the bottom end.

3 Place the smaller rectangle on the wrong side of the larger felt piece (figure 13). Line up the ends that are not stitched. Pin the pieces together at the bottom.

4 Firmly roll the felt around the pin (figure 14).

5 Carefully align the decorative stitching. Pin the bead closed (figure 15). Remove the inner pin.

6 Slip a needle, threaded with six strands of embroidery floss, under the pinned edge about ⅛ inch (3 mm) from one end and tightly wrap the floss around the bead.

7 Secure the floss by running the needle through the bead and out the end. Cut the floss close to the bead (figure 16).

8 Repeat steps 6 and 7 on the other side of the felt bead.

9 Trim the ends of the bead with scissors if necessary. Slipstitch the bead closed.

Figure 13

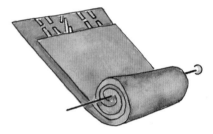

Figure 14

Figure 15

Figure 16

Making a Felt Tassel

What You Need

For purse tassels

3 x 3¼-inch (7.6 x 8.3 cm) piece of cardboard

5 yards (4.6 m) of yarn or floss for a 3¼-inch (8.3 cm) tassel

For bookmark tassels

3 x 2¼-inch (7.6 x 5.7 cm) piece of cardboard

3 yards (2.7 m) of yarn or floss for a 2¼-inch (5.7 cm) tassel

For both

12-inch (30.5 cm) cord, yarn, or floss for the hanging tassel

12-inch (30.5 cm) yarn or floss for the neck binding

Tapestry needle to fit the yarn or floss

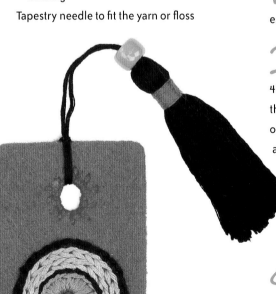

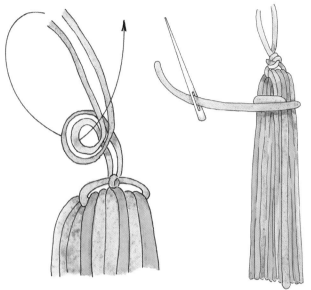

Figure 17   Figure 18   Figure 19

What You Do

1 Cut the cord, yarn, or floss for the hanging tassel to the desired length. Make a knot in each end to prevent unraveling.

2 Cut the cardboard to size and wrap the yarn or floss around it lengthwise about 40 times, depending on the desired fullness of the tassel you're making. Pile the wraps on top of each other, keeping the pile as narrow as possible.

3 Slip one end of the hanging cord between wrapped yarn and the cardboard. Tie a knot, pull the knot tight, and then slip the yarn off the board.

4 Hold the ends of the cord together and tie an overhand knot (figure 17). Leave the ends of the hanging cord loose.

5 Thread the yarn or floss for binding the tassel on a tapestry needle. Lay the end of the yarn at the bottom edge of the tassel, parallel to the tassel strands. Bring the end with the needle to ½ inch (1.3 cm) from the top and wrap it tightly around the tassel (figure 18). Keep each wrap parallel to the next, starting at the top and working down. Make at least five wraps. End by slipping the needle under the wraps and up through the top of the tassel and clip (figure 19).

6 Cut the hanging loops at the open end and trim evenly to the desired length.

7 Tie the tassel to the item with the hanging cord.

Basic Embroidery

Here is everything you need to know about hand embroidery.

Embroidery Threads

The projects in this book use either crewel wool or cotton embroidery floss. For some projects, you may choose to use either thread. We've provided colors and numbers for both Paternayan Persian wool yarn and DMC embroidery floss. If we've listed only one or the other, it's because that thread suits the design better. When you have a choice, the first thread listed is the thread we used for the project, the one shown in the photo.

When substituting threads, adapt the strands as follows:

1 strand wool = 6 strands floss

2 strands wool = 12 strands floss

Crewel wool gives embroidery a lush, rich look. It shows more texture than floss and is good for larger projects because it covers an area quickly. It comes in a beautiful array of colors and can be purchased at local stores or online. Paternayan wool is sold as three strands, which can be separated as indicated in the project instructions. It is sold in small skeins of 8 yards (7.3 m) and in larger hanks with the amount varying depending on the source. There are other brands of wool available, some of which are two-stranded. Most of the projects in this book use one strand of wool.

Cotton embroidery floss is a popular thread for embroidery, and rightly so. It's inexpensive, washable, and easy for beginners to handle. Plus, it comes in hundreds of colors. The two most popular manufacturers, DMC and Anchor, offer the greatest number of colors, while other companies specialize in unique threads, such as hand-dyed colors. Floss is sold in six-stranded skeins. Most designs in this book use six strands of floss.

Embroidery Tools

Embroidery needles are the most essential tools in embroidery. Poorly made needles have small imperfections, so buy the highest quality you can afford to ensure yourself a pleasurable stitching experience. The size of the needle is important. A needle that's too small might damage the thread because the thread won't slide easily through the eye. A needle that's too large might leave holes in the fabric and produce sloppy stitches. Buy a package of embroidery needles with several different sizes and slide the thread through the eye of a few different ones to find the right size. Keep in mind that the larger the needle number size, the smaller the eye of the needle.

Crewel needles are basic to embroidery. These average-length needles have long, oval eyes and sharp points for piercing fabric. Use crewel needles for all the designs in this book. A size 22 needle is a good size for most threads.

A thimble protects your middle fingertip as you stitch. It's a personal choice; some stitchers wouldn't stitch without one, while others find them distracting. Practice with a thimble to see

if you like it and don't give up right away. It takes time to get used to it.

A thread organizer keeps your embroidery threads clean and untangled. The simplest solution is a set of labeled, plastic resealable bags. If you do a lot of stitching, invest in a large, sectioned box designed just for stitchers.

Stretcher bars or hoops are frequently used in traditional embroidery to keep fabric taut during stitching. In this book, all the projects are stitched on felt, which might stretch when it is pulled, so stretcher bars and hoops are not used. Instead, hold the felt in your hands during embroidery.

Embroidery scissors are small and sharp. Keep them separate from your other scissors and only use them for embroidery so they stay clean and sharp. Keep them in a sheath to protect the points (and your hands!).

Embroidery Techniques

Here are the basic techniques you'll need to understand to embroider.

Separating floss or wool strands, also known as "plying," is often the first step. It separates and prepares the number of strands you need to stitch each area. Separating the strands before stitching helps them fluff out to cover the fabric better. Even if you intend to stitch with the remaining strands on your length of floss, separate and recombine them nevertheless.

To straighten the strands, locate a loose, cut end of a skein of six-stranded floss or three-stranded wool and cut a length not longer than 18 inches (45.7 cm). Hold the thread at one end and "fan out" the individual strands; select one strand and pull it out. Repeat with the remaining strands and straighten each one after each separation. Place the strands together and thread them through the needle.

Threading the needle is another vital skill. Pinch the floss ends together tightly between your thumb and forefinger (or thumb and middle finger) with fingernails touching, allowing the warmth of your fingers to press the floss ends as flat as possible. Roll your fingers back to expose the ends, and insert them into the needle's eye.

Securing the thread is necessary to begin and end a section of stitching. The debate among stitchers is whether to knot or not. Pro-knot-

ters suggest that if the design features raised effects, why not knot? Anti-knotters believe that embroidery should look as flat as possible, and consider knots undesirable. Feel free to decide for yourself.

Eliminating the starting knots will ensure a clean look. Use an in-line waste knot when you begin a new thread. Plan the direction you'll be stitching, make a knot, and insert it (from the top of the fabric) along that same path, but further ahead of the first stitch. Stitch over the thread and clip the knot off just before you reach it.

Sometimes using a knot is virtually unavoidable, such as when a French, Colonial, or Bullion Knot is isolated from other stitches. Try this nearly inconspicuous knot that appears as a tiny stitch on the right side of the fabric:

1 On the back of the fabric, pick up two (or so) fabric threads with the threaded needle to make the first stitch, leaving a ¼-inch (6 mm) thread tail.

2 Take a backstitch at the same spot, but at a right angle to the first stitch.

3 Take another backstitch at the same spot in the same direction as the second stitch.

Begin and end individual threads as neatly as possible, as some projects show the back of your stitching. Do not carry threads from one area to another unless the distance is ⅛ inch (3 mm) or less. Even if the back of your project will be concealed by the finishing treatment, it's a good idea to minimize carrying threads between areas, especially if you are using a light-colored fabric.

Correcting mistakes is inevitable. As you stitch, you are bound to make stitches that you want to correct. You may have executed the stitch sequence incorrectly or simply produced a stitch that looks less than lovely.

In the first case, it's a good idea to pull out the offending stitches and re-stitch. In the second case, use your best judgment, keeping in mind that embroidery is a hand-done art form that is not intended to look as "perfect" as machine-done work.

If the stitches in question are few and you are still using the same thread, simply remove the needle and, working on the back of the fabric, gently pull the thread back through the fabric as far as you need to, then re-thread the needle and continue stitching. However, if you need to remove more than a few stitches, you will stress the thread and possibly ruin its appearance by pulling it through the fabric so many times. In this case, it's best to discard that particular thread and re-stitch with a new thread.

Ending the thread is the final step. To end a thread, turn your work over and weave the thread in and out of completed stitches of the same color. If the stitches are long and loose on the back (as with satin stitches), take one or two backstitches into the backs of the stitches (not into the fabric) to secure the thread. Avoid weaving a dark-colored thread through the back of light-colored areas.

Embroidery Stitches

You don't have to memorize these stitches because as you do more embroidery, they will become more and more familiar to you. Until then, refer to the instructive illustrations starting on page 110.

Backstitch

Blanket Stitch

Chain Stitch

Feather Stitch

Fishbone Stitch

Fly Stitch

French Knot

Herringbone Stitch

Lazy Daisy

Long and Short Stitch

Outline Stitch

Palestrina Stitch

Running Stitch

Satin Stitch

Slipstitch

Straight Stitch

Whipped Spider Stitch

Whipped Stem Stitch

Whipstitch

Woven Picot

Bright Morning Pillow

With its bold colors, this pillow will delight you when you wake up. Rise and shine!

What You Need

Felt

Yellow, 18 x 22 inches (45.7 x 55.9 cm)

Medium blue, 16 x 18 inches (40.6 x 45.7 cm)

Orange, 6 x 6 inches (15.2 x 15.2 cm)

Dark blue, 10 x 10 inches (25.4 x 25.4 cm)

Medium pink, 4 x 4 inches (10.2 x 10.2 cm)

Decorative Thread

Paternayan yarn or DMC embroidery floss

Paternayan yarn

Pink (#962), 1 yard (91.4 cm)

Yellow (#770), 6 yards (5.5 m)

Green (#699), 1½ yards (1.4 m)

Blue (#552), ¾ yard (68.6 cm)

DMC embroidery floss

Pink (#961), 1 yard (91.4 cm)

Yellow (#972), 6 yards (5.5 m)

Green (#700), 1½ yards (1.4 m)

Blue (#322), ¾ yard (68.6 cm)

Other Supplies

Straight pins

Sewing needle

Sewing thread, invisible or matching felt colors

Basting spray (optional)

Sewing machine

Polyester fiberfill

Yellow outline stitch

What You Do

1 Cut the yellow felt to 16 x 18 inches (40.6 x 45.7 cm), the same size as the piece of medium blue felt.

2 Transfer the patterns on page 121 onto the felt, referring to the project photo for the correct colors. Cut them out.

3 Pin the orange shape A onto the yellow square. Pin the yellow square onto the dark blue felt. See the project photo for placement.

4 Pin the orange shape B onto the dark blue felt and slipstitch it in place with orange sewing thread.

5 Pin the finished dark blue felt piece onto the medium blue pillow top and slipstitch it in place with dark blue sewing thread.

6 Stitch the petal according to the project photo. Pin the flower to the pillow top at the opening in the border marking; slipstitch it in place with pink sewing thread.

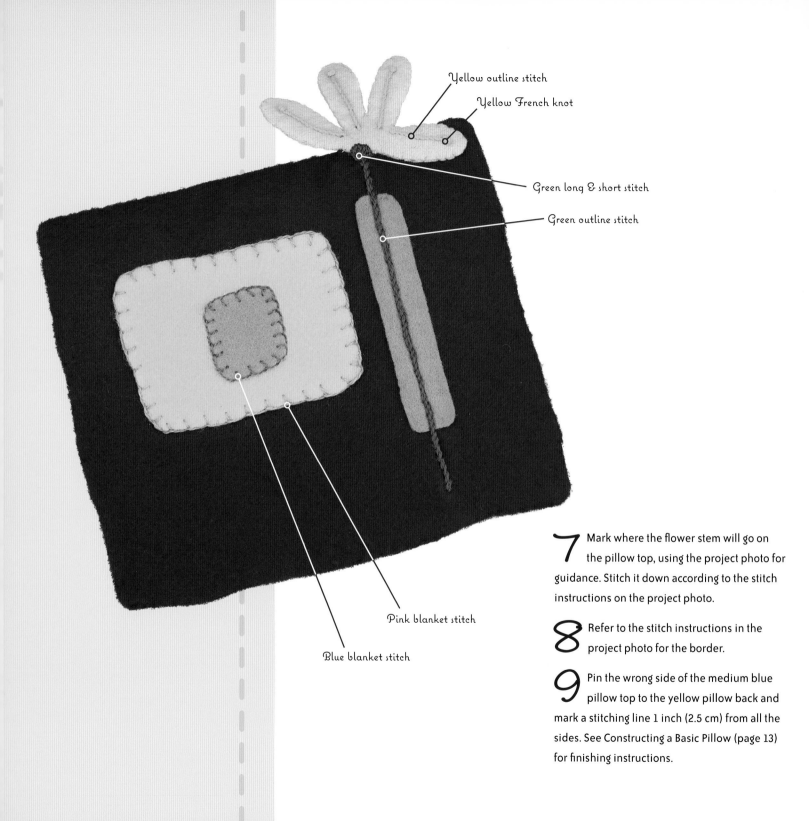

Yellow outline stitch

Yellow French knot

Green long & short stitch

Green outline stitch

Pink blanket stitch

Blue blanket stitch

7 Mark where the flower stem will go on the pillow top, using the project photo for guidance. Stitch it down according to the stitch instructions on the project photo.

8 Refer to the stitch instructions in the project photo for the border.

9 Pin the wrong side of the medium blue pillow top to the yellow pillow back and mark a stitching line 1 inch (2.5 cm) from all the sides. See Constructing a Basic Pillow (page 13) for finishing instructions.

Barrel Candy Bracelet

*This colorful, swirling felt bracelet—
set off by silver beads—will take years
off your attitude.*

What You Need

Felt, each 6 x 6 inches (15.2 x 15.2 cm)

Orange

Yellow

Medium blue

Fuchsia

Pink

Lime green

Red

Green

Purple

Decorative Thread

DMC embroidery floss, one skein each

Yellow (#726)

Fuchsia (#3607)

Orange (#3340)

Yellow Orange (#742)

Purple (#3837)

Lime Green (#166)

Turquoise (#3845)

Pink (#3832)

Other Supplies

9 silver beads, 5-mm

Elastic bracelet thread, 12 inches (30.5 cm)

Fabric glue

Straight pins

What You Do

1 Make four felt beads (page 16). Work with six strands of floss. Use one piece each of orange, yellow, blue, and fuchsia felt, 1¼ x 2 ¾ inches (3.2 x 7.0 cm) for the outside of the beads. Embroider these pieces as shown in the photos at right. Cut two pink felt pieces, one lime green piece, and one orange piece, 1¼ x 2³⁄₈ inches (3.2 x 6.0 cm) for the inside of the beads. Refer to the project photo.

2 Make five felt swirls (page 16). Cut the felt into ⅝ x 1½-inch (1.6 x 3.8 cm) pieces as follows: two pink, two red, two yellow, one lime green, one medium blue, one green, and one purple. Make two swirls with pink felt on the outside and red on the inside. Make one swirl with lime green on the outside and medium blue on the inside, one swirl with yellow on the outside and green on the inside, and one with purple on the outside and yellow on the inside.

3 Lay out the bracelet by lining up the felt beads, swirls, and silver beads in a pleasing pattern. Place a bead between each felt bead or swirl. Thread the elastic on the needle and run it through the center of the felt beads lengthwise and through the felt swirls so that the swirl design shows. Add or subtract a felt swirl to make the bracelet fit. Knot the elastic cord and bury the ends in a felt bead.

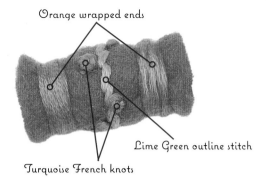

Orange wrapped ends

Lime Green outline stitch

Turquoise French knots

Fuchsia wrapped ends

Turquoise chain stitch

Yellow chain stitch

Fuchsia wrapped ends

Yellow Orange chain stitch

Orange outline stitch

Lime Green chain stitch

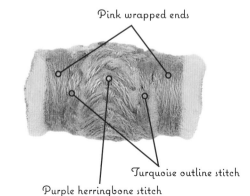

Pink wrapped ends

Turquoise outline stitch

Purple herringbone stitch

Twirling Flower Coasters

Plant these multi-colored coasters around your home to turn any season into springtime!

27

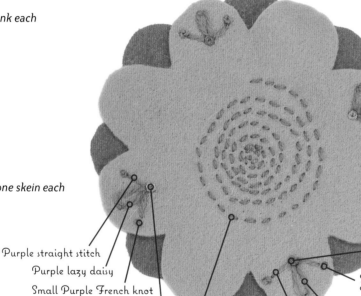

What You Need

Felt

Orange, 9 x 12 inches (22.9 x 30.5 cm)

Purple, 9 x 12 inches (22.9 x 30.5 cm)

Fuchsia, 9 x 12 inches (22.9 x 30.5 cm)

Green, 6 x 6 inches (15.2 x 15.2 cm)

Lime green, 6 x 6 inches (15.2 x 15.2 cm)

Decorative Thread

Paternayan yarn or DMC embroidery floss

Paternayan yarn, one hank each

Purple (#301)

Light Green (#698)

Turquoise (#592)

Yellow Orange (#812)

Fuchsia (#352)

Dark Pink (#943)

Yellow (#773)

DMC embroidery floss, one skein each

Purple (#3837)

Light Green (#703)

Turquoise (#3845)

Yellow Orange (#741)

Fuchsia (#3607)

Dark Pink (#3832)

Yellow (#726)

Other Supplies

Basting spray (optional)

Straight pins (optional)

What You Do

1 Transfer the flower shape to the felt using the pattern on page 117. Cut them out.

2 Refer to the project photos for the stitch instructions and placement. Each coaster is a little different. For the small French knots, use one strand of yarn or three strands of floss. For the large French knots, double it.

Yellow Orange lazy daisies

Large Light Green French knot

Turquoise running stitch

Light Green lazy daisies

Large Purple French knot

Large Yellow Orange French knot

Purple fly stitches

Fuchsia fly stitches

Large Yellow French knot

Yellow running stitch

Purple straight stitch

Purple lazy daisy

Small Purple French knot

Large Light Green French knot

Purple running stitch

Large Purple French knot

Small Turquoise French knot

Turquoise lazy daisy

Turquoise straight stitch

Small Dark Pink French knot

Dark Pink straight stitches

Large Turquoise French knot

Yellow Orange straight stitches

Small Yellow Orange French knot

Large Light Green French knot

Light Green running stitch

Spiral Illusion Electronics Carrier

Keep your phone or music player safe and in style with this modern art piece.

What You Need

Felt

2 pieces of lavender, 6 x 8 inches (15.2 x 20.3 cm)
and ¼ x 4 inches (6 mm x 10.2 cm)

2 pieces of lime green, 8 x 10 inches (20.3 x 25.4
cm) and ¼ x 4 inches (6 mm x 10.2 cm)

Yellow orange, 3½ x 3½ inches (8.9 x 8.9 cm)

Decorative Thread

DMC embroidery floss, one skein each

Orange (#970)

Turquoise (#3845)

Green (#907)

Fuchsia (#3607)

Other Supplies

Fabric glue

Straight pins

Basting spray (optional)

Gold ring, 1 inch (2.5 cm) in diameter

Lavender chain (optional)

What You Do

1 Transfer the patterns on page 130 onto the felt as follows: two fronts to the lavender felt; two backs, one strap, and one medium-sized circle to the lime green felt; and one large circle to the yellow orange felt. Cut them out.

2 Refer to the stitch instructions on the project photo for the holder front.

3 Attach the circular yellow orange shape and the lime green circle according to the project photo.

4 Make a felt swirl with the lavender and lime green felt strips (page 16). Glue the swirl on the lime green circle. Refer to the project photo to complete the stitching.

5 Pin or use basting spray to hold the two lime green back pieces together. Thread the lime green strip of felt through the gold ring and fold the felt in half. Pin the strip in the center of the lime green pieces so the fold (and gold ring) is just above the top edge. Backstitch across the top of the strip just under the gold ring with Green floss, going through all the layers. Backstitch an "X" at the bottom of the strip with Green floss. Blanket stitch the edges of the strip to the back with Green floss.

6 With the wrong sides together, pin or spray baste the lavender pieces together. Pin the lavender pieces to the lime green pieces with wrong sides together. Blanket stitch the two lavender pieces together and the two lime green pieces together across the top only with Fuchsia floss. Then blanket stitch the four pieces together on the sides and bottom with Fuchsia floss.

7 Thread the chain through the gold ring.

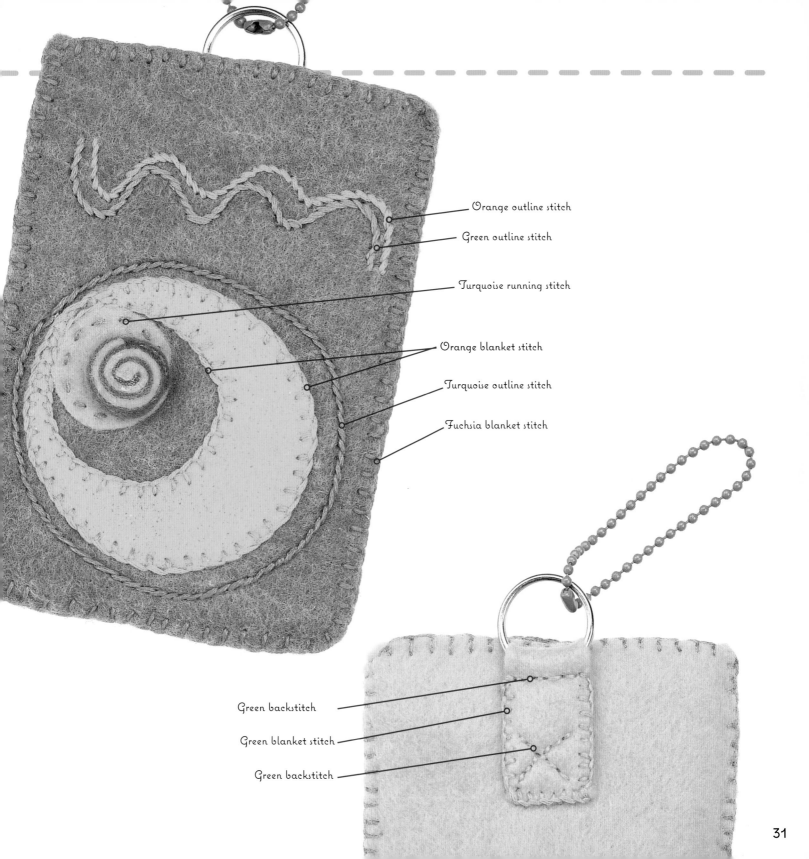

Orange outline stitch

Green outline stitch

Turquoise running stitch

Orange blanket stitch

Turquoise outline stitch

Fuchsia blanket stitch

Green backstitch

Green blanket stitch

Green backstitch

I ♥ Books Bookmark

This sweet little project makes a great gift to remind your friends who loves them: you.

What You Need

Felt

Orange, 6 x 6 inches (15.2 x 15.2 cm)

Pink, 6 x 6 inches (15.2 x 15.2 cm)

Purple, 3 x 3 inches (7.6 x 7.6 cm)

Decorative Thread

DMC embroidery floss, one skein each

Turquoise (#3845)

Lime Green (#166)

Dark Pink (#956)

Light Pink (#963)

Other Supplies

Sewing needle

Sewing thread, orange or invisible

1-inch (2.5 cm) wide pink grosgrain ribbon,

9 inches (22.9 cm) in length

Fabric glue

17 turquoise 2-mm beads

Orange 5-mm bead

Cardboard, 3 x 1¼ inches (7.6 x 3.2 cm)

What You Do

1 Transfer the shapes onto the felt using the patterns on page 128. Cut them out.

2 Refer to the stitch instructions in the project photo.

3 Attach the orange circle to the pink heart shape according to the photo detail.

4 Cut a point on one end of the ribbon by folding it in half and cutting on an angle. Stitch the other end to the center of the orange heart with three strands of Dark Pink floss.

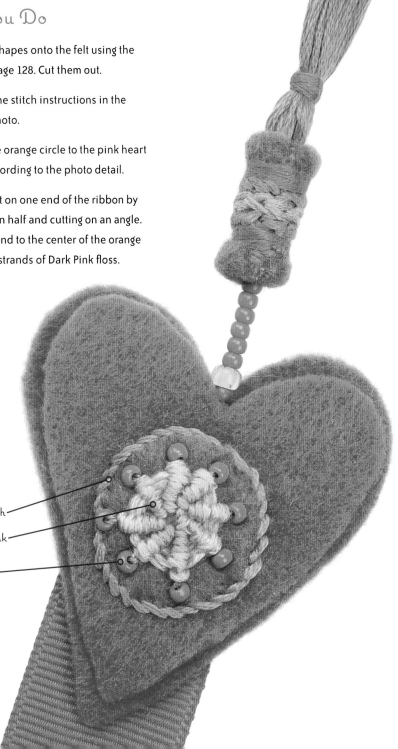

Lime Green outline stitch

Light Pink & Dark Pink whipped spider stitch

Turquoise beads

5   Apply glue on the center back of the pink heart and center the pink heart on top of the orange heart. Let the glue dry.

6   Make a felt bead (page 16). Cut one piece of orange felt 1 x 2 inches (2.5 x 5.1 cm) and one piece of pink felt 1 x 1⅛ inches (2.5 x 2.9 cm). Embroider two-thirds of the orange felt: Chain stitch with Dark Pink floss down the center. Then outline stitch a line on each side of the chain stitch with Lime Green floss. Finish the bead as described on page 16. Use Turquoise floss to whip around the ends of the bead. Trim the ends if necessary.

7   Make a tassel (page 17) that is about 1¼ inches (3.2 cm) long with Lime Green floss for the tassel and Turquoise floss around the neck. Allow two tails of turquoise floss to become part of the tassel.

8   To attach the tassel to the bookmark, cut three strands of Lime Green floss about 6 inches (15.2 cm) long and knot one end. Thread the other end of the floss through the top of the tassel and then through the felt bead. Add 6 turquoise beads next to the felt bead, then the orange bead, followed by 3 more turquoise beads. Run the floss between the orange and pink hearts and bring the needle out the back of the orange heart. Pull the floss taut so the beads are snug, and stitch the ends of the floss securely to the back of the orange heart.

9   Glue the turquoise heart to the center of the back of the orange heart to cover the stitches.

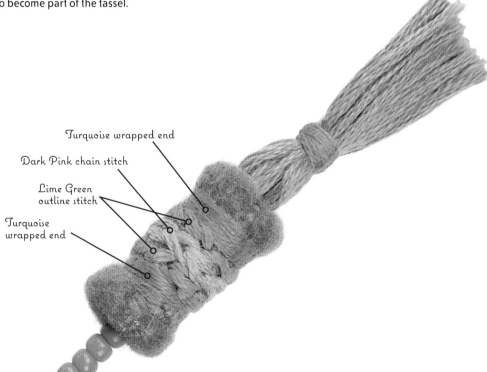

Turquoise wrapped end

Dark Pink chain stitch

Lime Green outline stitch

Turquoise wrapped end

Spring Blossom Pincushion

This flowery accessory will bring springtime into your craft corner all year round.

What You Need

Felt

Lime green, 4 x 4 inches (10.2 x 10.2 cm)

Pink, 4 x 4 inches (10.2 x 10.2 cm)

Yellow orange, 3½ x 3½ inches (8.9 x 8.9 cm)

Blue, 3 x 3 inches (7.6 x 7.6 cm)

Decorative Thread

DMC embroidery floss, 1 yard (91.4 cm) each

Green (#907)

Turquoise (#3846)

Purple (#209)

Dark Pink (#602)

Yellow Orange (#742)

Other Supplies

Sewing needle

Sewing thread in lime green, yellow, and blue

Polyester fiberfill

Lightweight cardboard, 2½ inches (6.4 cm) square

Fabric glue

What You Do

1 Transfer the shapes onto the felt using the patterns on page 125 as follows: two pink felt flowers and one yellow orange felt flower center. In addition, measure out one lime green felt 4-inch (10.2 cm) diameter circle. Cut out all the shapes.

2 Refer to Constructing a Pincushion on page 15 for further instructions. Use matching floss where appropriate. For the pincushion base, cut out a 1¾-inch (4.5 cm) circle from the lightweight cardboard. Cut out a 2¾ inches (7.0 cm) diameter circle of blue felt.

3 Stitch the yellow orange felt circles according to the project photo. After you've stuffed it according to the instructions on page 15, set it aside until later.

4 Pin both flower shapes, one on top of the other, to the pincushion body, and then stitch them down per the project photo. Then glue and whipstitch the flower center (the stuffed yellow orange piece) over the top of the pincushion, at the center of the flower. Refer to the project photo.

5 Add the border on the lower edge.

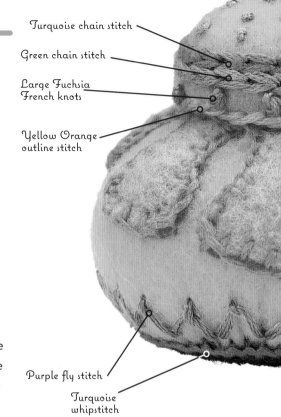

Turquoise chain stitch

Green chain stitch

Large Fuchsia French knots

Yellow Orange outline stitch

Purple fly stitch

Turquoise whipstitch

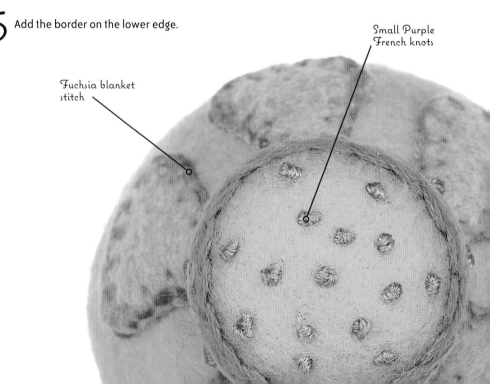

Small Purple French knots

Fuchsia blanket stitch

Pretty Kitty Appliqué

This feline friend will find its way into your heart and onto your belongings.

What You Need

Felt

Black, 6 x 8 inches (15.2 x 20.3 cm)

White, 3 x 4 inches (7.6 x 10.2 cm)

Gold, 2 x 2 inches (5.1 x 5.1 cm)

Light pink, 2 x 2 inches (5.1 x 5.1 cm)

Decorative Thread

DMC embroidery floss or Paternayan yarn

DMC embroidery floss, one skein each

White (Blanc)

Variegated Pink (#112)

Fuchsia (#3806)

Pink (#603)

Turquoise (#3845)

Medium Fuchsia (#3607)

Yellow (#743)

Green (#906)

Paternayan yarn, 1 yard (91.4 cm) each

White (#206)

Variegated Pink (#903)

Fuchsia (#903)

Pink (#962)

Turquoise (#592)

Medium Fuchsia (#903)

Yellow (#712)

Green (#698)

Other Supplies

Basting spray (optional)

What You Do

1 Transfer the shapes and stitch patterns to the felt using the patterns on page 120. Cut them out.

2 Stitch the collar onto the cat, following the stitches indicated in the project photo.

3 Stitch the cat's face, according to the stitches indicated in the project photo and photo detail.

4 Pin the felt eyelids in place over each eye. Blanket stitch around each outside curve with White floss.

5 Place the mouse under the collar. Attach the mouse to the cat with a Turquoise French knot at the eye location. Create the mouse's tail by outline stitching in Turquoise. Add the hanger with a Medium Fuchsia straight stitch, adding a French knot at the end.

6 Attach the cat appliqué to the item with a Variegated Pink blanket stitch.

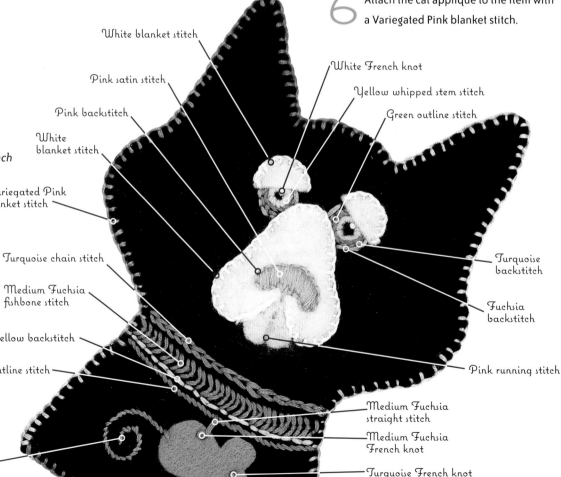

White blanket stitch

Pink satin stitch

Pink backstitch

White blanket stitch

Variegated Pink blanket stitch

Turquoise chain stitch

Medium Fuchsia fishbone stitch

Yellow backstitch

Green outline stitch

Turquoise outline stitch

White French knot

Yellow whipped stem stitch

Green outline stitch

Turquoise backstitch

Fuchsia backstitch

Pink running stitch

Medium Fuchsia straight stitch

Medium Fuchsia French knot

Turquoise French knot

Rainbow Band Bracelet

This bright bangle will show off your stitching and dazzle your friends.

What You Need

Felt

Fuchsia, 12 x 4 inches (30.5 x 10.2 cm)

Decorative Thread

DMC embroidery floss, 1 yard (91.4 cm) each

Yellow Orange (#742)

Orange (#970)

Green (#704)

Purple (#208)

Turquoise (#996)

Light Fuchsia (#3609)

Other Supplies

Strip of 14-count plastic canvas, 12 x 1¼ inches
(30.5 x 3.2 cm), or a piece of Buckram, 12 x 3¾
inches (30.5 x 9.5 cm)

Sewing needle

Sewing thread, invisible or matching felt

Straight pins

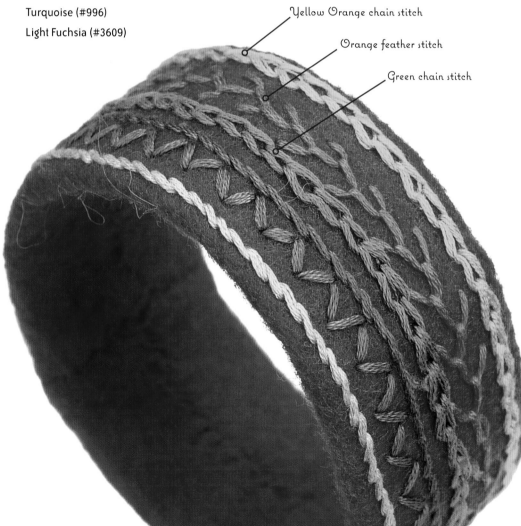

Yellow Orange chain stitch

Orange feather stitch

Green chain stitch

What You Do

1 Measure your wrist and add 4 to 5 inches (10.2 to 12.7 cm) so the bracelet will slip over your hand. Cut the piece of 14-count plastic canvas or Buckram to this length. If you are using plastic canvas, overlap the short ends by 1 inch (2.5 cm) and stitch them firmly closed using floss or strong thread. If you're using Buckram, fold it in thirds lengthwise to provide more stiffness before overlapping and stitching. This piece should be able to slip over your hand. Set the piece aside.

2 Cut the fuchsia felt $2\frac{1}{2}$ inches (6.4 cm) wide by the length of the bracelet from step 1, plus $\frac{1}{4}$ inch (6 mm).

3 Copy the stitching lines onto the felt using the project photo as a reference.

4 Refer to the stitch instructions on the project photo.

5 Center the embroidered felt, wrong side down, over the plastic bracelet and turn under one short end $\frac{1}{8}$ inch (3 mm). Position the folded felt edge away from the overlapped plastic or Buckram ends to minimize bulk and slipstitch it to the bracelet with matching sewing thread.

6 Bring the other short end around to the folded, stitched-down edge. Fold this end under so that the felt is taut and slipstitch it down right next to the first folded edge.

7 Wrap the sides to the inside of the bracelet. Make sure the felt is taut; trim it if necessary to smooth the right side. Pin it down and ladder stitch the edges together with matching sewing thread.

Purple outline stitch

Turquoise straight stitch in a zigzag pattern

Light Fuchsia outline stitch

Night and Day Hobo Bag

This stylish shoulder bag makes
it easy to get up and go.
It's hobo-chic!

French knot

Straight stitch

Satin stitch

Backstitch

Whipped stem stitch

Chain stitch

What You Need

Felt

Navy blue, 25 x 36 inches (63.5 x 91.4 cm)

Rust, 25 x 36 inches (63.5 x 91.4 cm)

Decorative Thread

Paternayan yarn or DMC embroidery floss

Paternayan yarn, 6 yards (5.5 m) each

Rust (#403)

Navy (#502)

DMC embroidery floss, 2 skeins each

Rust (#921)

Navy (#312)

Other Supplies

Sewing thread, rust and blue

Straight pins

Sewing machine (optional)

What You Do

1 Use the hobo bag pattern on page 130 (at the correct size) to cut out four pieces of the blue felt and four pieces of the rust felt.

2 Transfer the stitch design (page 119) onto one piece of the rust felt. Flop or reverse the stitch design, and transfer it onto the navy felt so that the designs mirror each other when placed side by side. Center the design on each piece of felt, with ½ inch (1.3 cm) between the inside edge of the design and the cut edge of the felt. See the project photo for reference.

3 Refer to the stitch instructions on the project photo. Use the Navy yarn or floss on the rust felt and the Rust yarn or floss on the navy blue felt.

4 Use the instructions for Constructing a Hobo Bag on page 13 to finish the bag from the eight pieces of felt.

Book Buddy Blossom

You'll never lose your place again with this pretty project popping out of your paperback.

What You Need

Felt

Purple, 3 x 8 inches (7.6 x 20.3 cm)

Green, 3 x 8 inches (7.6 x 20.3 cm)

Fuchsia, 4 x 4 inches (10.2 x 10.2 cm)

Yellow Orange, 2 x 2 inches (5.1 x 5.1 cm)

Orange, 2 x 2 inches (5.1 x 5.1 cm)

Decorative Thread

Paternayan yarn or DMC embroidery floss

Paternayan yarn, 1 yard (91.4 cm) each

Light Green (#698)

Orange (#811)

Turquoise (#592)

DMC embroidery floss, one skein each

Light Green (#703)

Orange (#947)

Turquoise (#3845)

Other Supplies

Fabric glue or fusible web (light or medium
weight)

Straight pins

Sewing needle

Sewing thread, invisible or gold

9 gold glass 5-mm beads

Basting spray (optional)

What You Do

1 Transfer the shapes to the felt using the patterns on page 127, as follows: one yellow orange and one orange circle, one green and one purple bookmark shape, and one fuchsia flower shape. Cut them out.

2 Refer to the stitch instructions in the project photo.

3 Glue or use fusible web (following the package instructions) to attach the green bookmark-sized felt to the back of the purple bookmark-sized felt. Pin the fuchsia flower on top of the purple bookmark and then glue or backstitch it in place.

4 Chain stitch a ⅝-inch (1.6 cm) diameter circle in the center of the yellow orange circle with Turquoise yarn or floss. Refer to the detail photo for more instructions. Sew the beads in the center of the flower.

5 Glue or fuse the other orange circle to the back of the flower. Blanket stitch the edge.

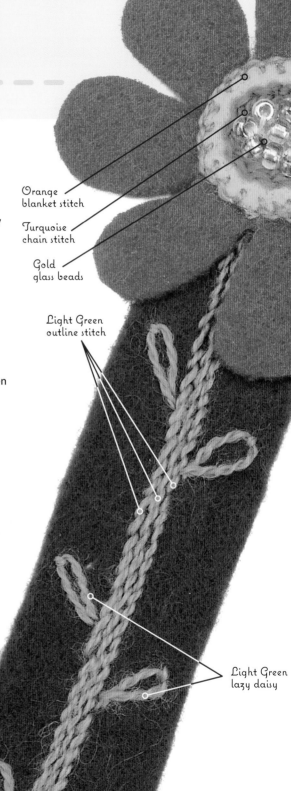

Orange
blanket stitch

Turquoise
chain stitch

Gold
glass beads

Light Green
outline stitch

Light Green
lazy daisy

45

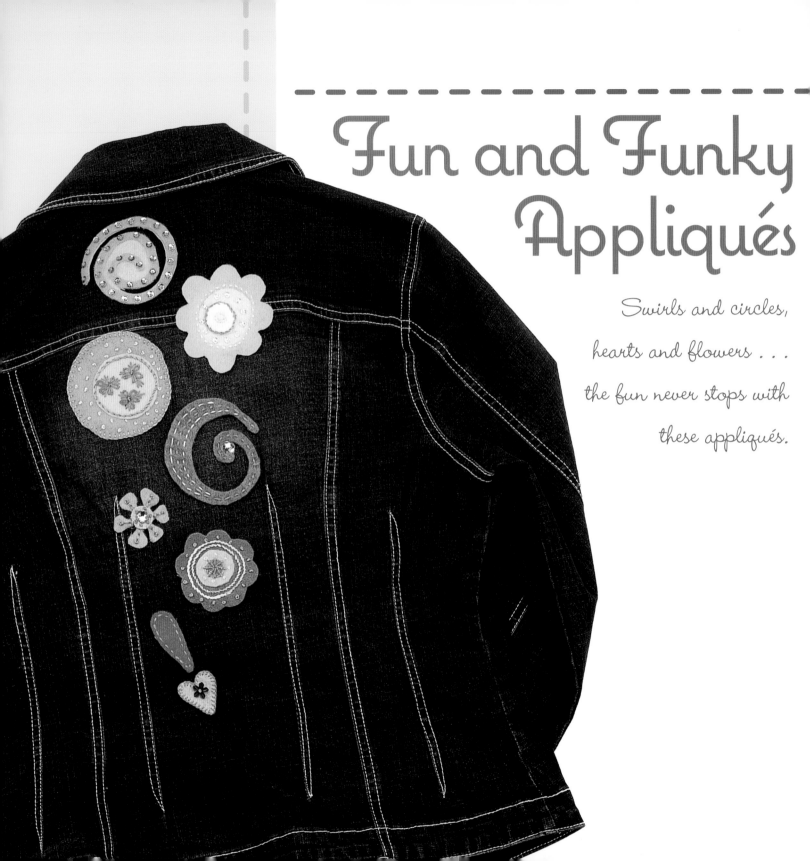

Fun and Funky Appliqués

Swirls and circles,

hearts and flowers . . .

the fun never stops with

these appliqués.

What You Need

Lime Green Flower

Felt

Lime green, 4 x 4 inches (10.2 x 10.2 cm)

Pale blue, 3 x 3 inches (7.6 x 7.6 cm)

Pale pink, 2 x 2 inches (5.1 x 5.1 cm)

Decorative Thread

DMC embroidery floss, one skein each

Light Fuchsia (#3609)

Turquoise (#3845)

Light Yellow (#744)

Other Supplies

11 crystal 5-mm beads

Gold Flower

Felt

Gold, 3 x 3 inches (7.6 x 7.6 cm)

Dusty blue, 2 x 2 inches (5.1 x 5.1 cm)

Decorative Thread

DMC embroidery floss, one skein each

Blue Purple (#3746)

Dark Fuchsia (#3804)

Other Supplies

Blue acrylic 10-mm jewel

Fabric glue

Purple Flower

Felt

Purple, 3 x 3 inches (7.6 x 7.6 cm)

Lime green, 2 x 2 inches (5.1 x 5.1 cm)

Decorative Thread

DMC embroidery floss, one skein each

Variegated Fuchsia (#116)

Variegated Yellow (#90)

Blue Green (#3851)

Orange Swirl

Felt

Orange, 4 x 4 inches (10.2 x 10.2 cm)

Lime green, 4 x 4 inches (10.2 x 10.2 cm)

Decorative Thread

DMC embroidery floss, one skein each

Turquoise (#3845)

Other Supplies

24 turquoise sequins

10 bright pink sequins

Basting spray

Small, sharp scissors

Brown Swirl

Felt

Brown, 4 x 4 inches
(10.2 x 10.2 cm)

Decorative Thread

DMC embroidery floss, one
skein each

Turquoise (#3845)

Light Fuchsia (#3609)

Other Supplies

Pink acrylic 10-mm jewel

Fabric glue

Orange Circle

Felt

Orange, 4 x 4 inches (10.2 x 10.2 cm)

Bright pink, 3 x 3 inches (7.6 x 7.6 cm)

Decorative Thread

DMC embroidery floss, one skein each

Pink (#602)

Light Pink (#604)

Dark Fuchsia (#3804)

Green (#906)

Blue Purple (#3746)

Pink Exclamation

Felt

Fuchsia, 2 x 3 inches (5.1 x 7.6 cm)

Bright pink, 2 x 2 inches (5.1 x 5.1 cm)

Decorative Thread

DMC embroidery floss, one skein each

Turquoise (#3845)

Dark Fuchsia (#3804)

Other Supplies

Fuchsia flower-shaped sequin

All Appliqués

Other Supplies

Straight pins

Sewing needle and thread

Sewing machine (optional)

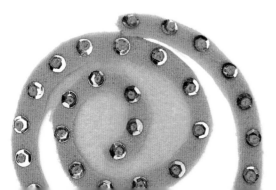

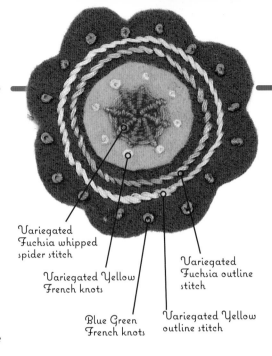

What You Do

Lime Green Flower

1. Transfer the shapes (page 126) onto the felt. Cut them out. Cut out a 1-inch (2.5 cm) diameter circle out of the center of the lime green flower shape.

2. Pin the pale blue circle behind the green flower and follow the stitching in the project photo to attach it.

3. Slipstitch or machine-stitch the appliqué to the item with matching thread.

Variegated Fuchsia whipped spider stitch

Variegated Yellow French knots

Variegated Fuchsia outline stitch

Blue Green French knots

Variegated Yellow outline stitch

Purple Flower

1. Transfer the shapes onto the felt using the patterns on page 126. Cut them out.

2. Refer to the stitch instructions in the project photo.

3. Attach the purple flower appliqué to the item.

Orange Swirl

1. Transfer the shapes onto the felt using the patterns on page 126, and cut them out.

2. Place orange swirl on top of the lime green circle. Starting at the outside edge of the swirl, attach the 24 turquoise sequins to the swirl with Turquoise French knots. Attach the 10 bright pink sequins, starting in the center of the swirl, with more Turquoise French knots.

3. Cut away the undecorated area of the lime green felt with the small, sharp scissors. Slipstitch the appliqué to the item with matching thread.

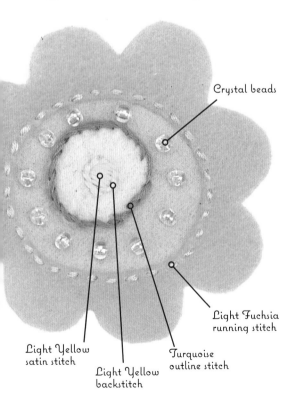

Crystal beads

Light Fuchsia running stitch

Light Yellow satin stitch

Light Yellow backstitch

Turquoise outline stitch

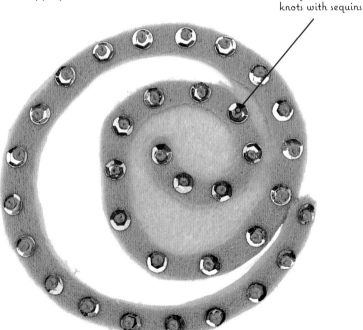

Turquoise French knots with sequins

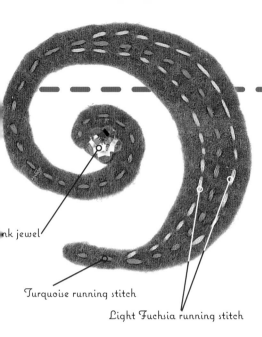

nk jewel

Turquoise running stitch

Light Fuchsia running stitch

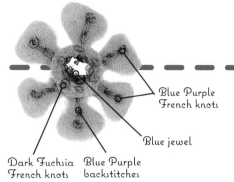

Blue Purple
French knots

Blue jewel

Dark Fuchsia   Blue Purple
French knots   backstitches

Brown Swirl

1 Transfer the swirl shape on page 126 to the felt. Cut it out.

2 Refer to the stitch instructions in the project photo.

3 Glue the pink jewel in the center of the appliqué. Slipstitch the appliqué to the item with matching thread.

Orange Circle

1 Transfer the shapes and stitch patterns onto the felt using the patterns on page 126, and cut them out.

2 Refer to the project photo for instructions.

3 Attach the pink felt circle to the orange circle using a Blue Purple outline stitch.

4 Attach the appliqué to the item with a Pink floss blanket stitch.

Gold Flower

1 Transfer the shapes and stitch patterns onto the felt using the patterns on page 126. Cut them out.

2 Refer to the project photo for instructions.

3 Glue the jewel in the center. Slipstitch the appliqué to the item with gold thread.

Pink Exclamation

1 Transfer the shapes onto the felt using the patterns on page 126, and cut them out.

2 Blanket stitch the heart appliqué to the item with Dark Fuchsia floss. Position the fuchsia shape above the heart and attach it with a Turquoise running stitch.

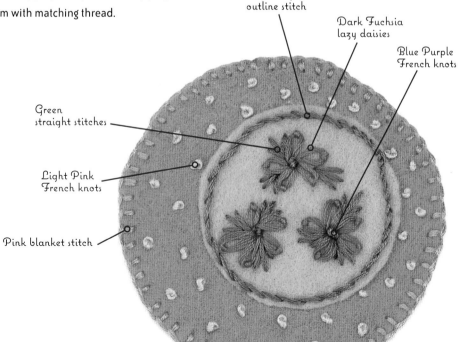

Blue Purple
outline stitch

Dark Fuchsia
lazy daisies

Blue Purple
French knots

Green
straight stitches

Light Pink
French knots

Pink blanket stitch

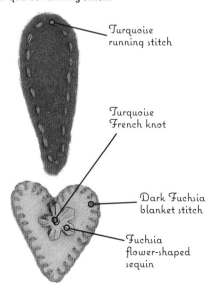

Turquoise
running stitch

Turquoise
French knot

Dark Fuchsia
blanket stitch

Fuchsia
flower-shaped
sequin

Green Garden Headrest

After a day in the garden, relax with this half-pillow. You'll never find a weed here!

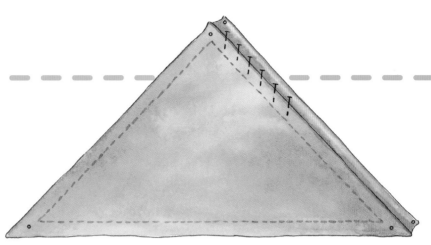

Figure 1

What You Need

Felt

Green, 20 x 20 inches (50.8 x 50.8 cm)

Fuchsia, 12 x 25 inches (30.5 x 63.5 cm)

Yellow orange, 3 x 3 inches (7.6 x 7.6 cm)

Decorative Thread

Paternayan yarn or DMC embroidery floss

Paternayan yarn

Light Yellow (#773), 3 yards (2.7 m)

Light Orange (#814), 2 yards (1.8 m)

Pale Blue (#544), 2 yards (1.8 m)

Light Green (#698), 2 yards (1.8 m)

Green (#699), 4 yards (3.7 m)

Turquoise (#592), 2 yards (1.8 m)

Purple (#301), 5 yards (4.6 m)

DMC embroidery floss

Light Yellow (#727), 3 yards (2.7 m)

Light Orange (#3825), 2 yards (1.8 m)

Pale Blue (#519), 2 yards (1.8 m)

Light Green (#703), 2 yards (1.8 m)

Green (#700), 4 yards (3.7 m)

Turquoise (#3845), 2 yards (1.8 m)

Purple (#208), 5 yards (4.6 m)

Other Supplies

Sewing needle

Sewing thread, invisible or matching felt colors

Sewing machine

Basting spray (optional)

Fabric marking pen

Straight pins

Polyester fiberfill

What You Do

1 Cut a 16-inch (40.6 cm) square from the green felt. Then cut the square diagonally into two triangles. Cut the pillow sides from fuchsia felt as follows: two strips 2½ x 16 inches (6.4 x 40.6 cm) and one strip 2½ x 22 inches (6.4 x 55.9 cm).

2 Transfer the flower petal shapes from the pattern on page 130 onto the fuchsia felt three times. Transfer the flower center shapes from the pattern onto the yellow orange felt three times. Cut them all out.

3 Mark a 1-inch (2.5 cm) border in from all sides of one green triangle (the pillow front). Stitch along that line with Fuchsia yarn or floss, as shown in the detail photo (page 52).

4 Place the flower centers on the fuchsia flowers. Stitch the flower petals, referring to detail photo for instructions. Add the swirls and French knots, as indicated. Stitch the stems and leaves on the green felt pillow front, as shown in the detail photo.

5 Place one flower on the pillow top at the top of each stem, in the order shown. Blanket stitch the flower borders.

6 Measure ½ inch (1.3 cm) from the corners of all the pieces and mark them with a fabric marking pen. Pin one short fuchsia strip to one short side of the pillow front with wrong sides together, matching the corner markings (figure 1). Stitch ½ inch (1.3 cm) from the edge, starting and stopping at the corner markings. Repeat with the other short side of the pillow front and the other short fuchsia strip.

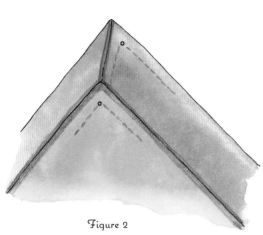

Figure 2

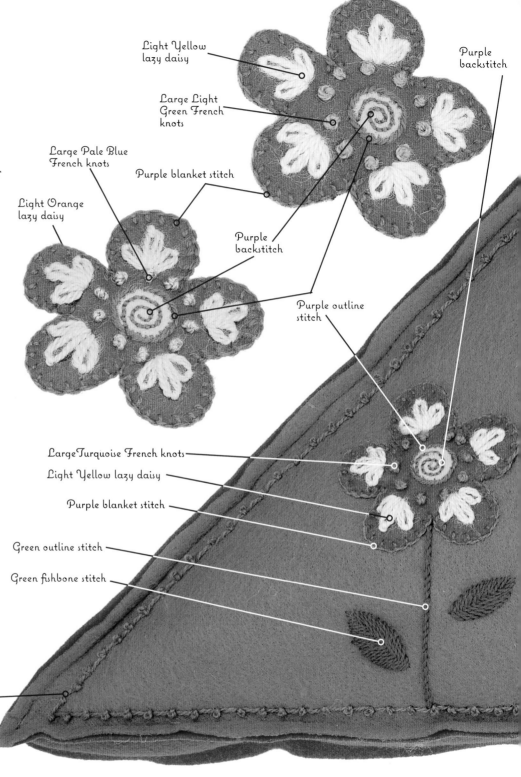

7 Stitch the short sides of the pillow back to the unstitched sides of the fuchsia strips, as in step 6.

8 At the top or peak of the pillow, stitch the fuchsia strips together ½ inch (1.3 cm) from the edges with wrong sides together to close the top of the pillow (figure 2).

9 Pin the long fuchsia strip to the bottom of the pillow front, matching the corner markings and with wrong sides together. Stitch ½ inch (1.3 cm), starting and stopping at the markings. Repeat for the back, but don't close the pillow completely. Leave an opening for stuffing the center. Stitch both triangle points as in step 8.

10 Stuff the pillow and sew the opening closed. Trim the excess felt away from the corners.

Light Yellow lazy daisy

Large Light Green French knots

Large Pale Blue French knots

Purple blanket stitch

Light Orange lazy daisy

Purple backstitch

Purple backstitch

Purple outline stitch

LargeTurquoise French knots

Light Yellow lazy daisy

Purple blanket stitch

Green outline stitch

Green fishbone stitch

Fuchsia palestrina stitch

Fairy Tale Fantasy Pincushion

Cinderella would have loved
this fanciful pincushion.
You will, too!

What You Need

Felt

Purple, 4 x 4 inches (10.2 x 10.2 cm)

Sage green, 4 x 4 inches (10.2 x 10.2 cm)

Fuchsia, 6 x 6 inches (15.2 x 15.2 cm)

Blue lavender, 6 x 6 inches (15.2 x 15.2 cm)

Gold, 2 x 2 inches (5.1 x 5.1 cm)

Decorative Thread

DMC embroidery floss, 1 yard (91.4 cm) each

    Fuchsia (#601)

    Gold (#728)

    Purple (#208)

Other Supplies

Sewing needle

Sewing thread, blue lavender and fuchsia

Polyester fiberfill

Lightweight cardboard, 2 x 2 inches

    (5.1 x 5.1 cm)

Fabric glue

Curved needle (optional)

What You Do

1 Transfer the shapes onto the felt using the patterns on page 121. Cut them out. Refer to the project photo for stitching instructions.

2 Follow the project photo to complete the stitching on the blue lavender felt circle and on the gold felt circle.

3 Refer to Constructing a Pincushion on page 15 for finishing instructions. Use matching floss where appropriate. For the pincushion base, cut out a 1½-inch (3.8 cm) diameter circle from the lightweight cardboard. Cut out a 2¼-inch (5.8 cm) diameter circle of fuchsia felt.

4 Attach the gold circle at the top center of the pincushion.

5 Apply a thin line of fabric glue to the base and place the pincushion on top. Let the glue set, and then blanket stitch the body to the base with the Fuchsia floss.

6 Blanket stitch around the outside edges of the two scalloped felt pieces, referring to the project photo.

7 Center and glue the bottom of the pincushion to the fuchsia shape. Center and glue the fuchsia shape (with pincushion attached) on top of the sage green felt. Center and glue the sage green felt on the purple felt so that the scallops are offset as in the project photo. Secure all the layers to the pincushion with a Fuchsia running stitch. Use a curved needle if you have one; it's easier to stitch through multiple layers with a curved needle.

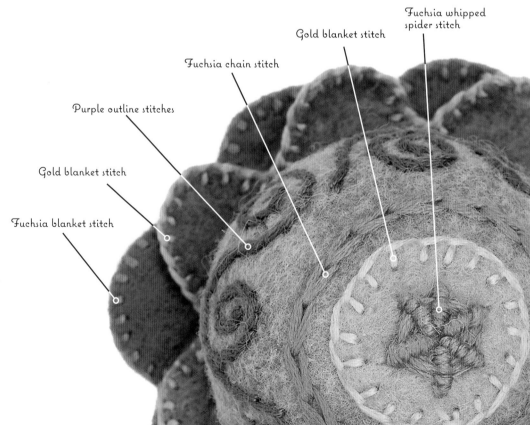

Fuchsia whipped spider stitch

Gold blanket stitch

Fuchsia chain stitch

Purple outline stitches

Gold blanket stitch

Fuchsia blanket stitch

Heartwarming Electronics Holster

Wear your heart in plain sight while protecting your phone or music player.

What You Need

Felt

2 pieces of pink, 4 x 4 inches (10. 2 x 10.2 cm)
and ⅝ x 4 inches (1.6 x 10.2 cm)

Lime green, 10 x 10 inches (25.4 x 25.4 cm)

Turquoise, 10 x 10 inches (25.4 x 25.4 cm)

Lavender, ¾ x 2 inches (1.9 x 5.1 cm)

2 pieces of fuchsia, 2 x 4 inches (5.1 x 10.2 cm)
and ⅝ x 4 inches (1.6 x 10.2 cm)

Orange, ¾ x 2 inches (1.9 x 5.1 cm)

Decorative Thread

DMC embroidery floss, one skein each

Fuchsia (#3607)

Green (#907)

Yellow Orange (#741)

Other Supplies

Fabric glue

Straight pins

Basting spray (optional)

Pink button, ½ inch (1.3 cm) in diameter

Sewing thread, invisible

Sewing needle (optional)

What You Do

1 Transfer the patterns on page 126 onto the felt and cut them out. Transfer the buttonhole marking on the back as indicated.

2 Blanket stitch the pink heart onto the lime green front. Refer to the project photo for placement.

3 Pin the turquoise strip onto the lime green front and hold it in place by stitching a French knot at each end with Fuchsia floss.

4 Make felt rolls from the lavender, fuchsia, and orange pieces of felt. Roll the lavender felt tightly into a log and wrap Green floss around each end, leaving a gap between the two thread wrappings. Secure the floss with tiny backstitches under the thread. Repeat with the Yellow Orange floss on wrapped fuchsia felt and the Fuchsia floss on wrapped orange felt.

5 Place the three felt rolls on top of the turquoise strip and backstitch them in place from the rear with Turquoise floss or sewing thread.

6 Make a felt swirl with the pink and fuchsia strips (page 16). Glue the finished swirl on the heart. Refer to the project photo for placement.

7 Pin or use basting spray to hold the turquoise and lime green back pieces together, with the turquoise felt on the inside. Cut a slit in the center of the buttonhole marking through both layers. Blanket stitch around the opening with Green floss. Keep your stitches close together so the buttonhole doesn't stretch.

8 With the lime green side on top, pin the two fronts together, and then blanket stitch them along every edge with Green floss.

9 With the turquoise side on top, pin the two backs together. Blanket stitch them completely with Green floss, including around the strap.

10 Place the front (lime green side up) on top of the back (turquoise side up). Line them up and pin them in place. Fold the strap to the front and mark the button location. Sew on the button on at the marking.

11 Blanket stitch the sides and bottom of the four pieces with Green floss, beginning and ending the stitching ½ inch (1.3 cm) from the top.

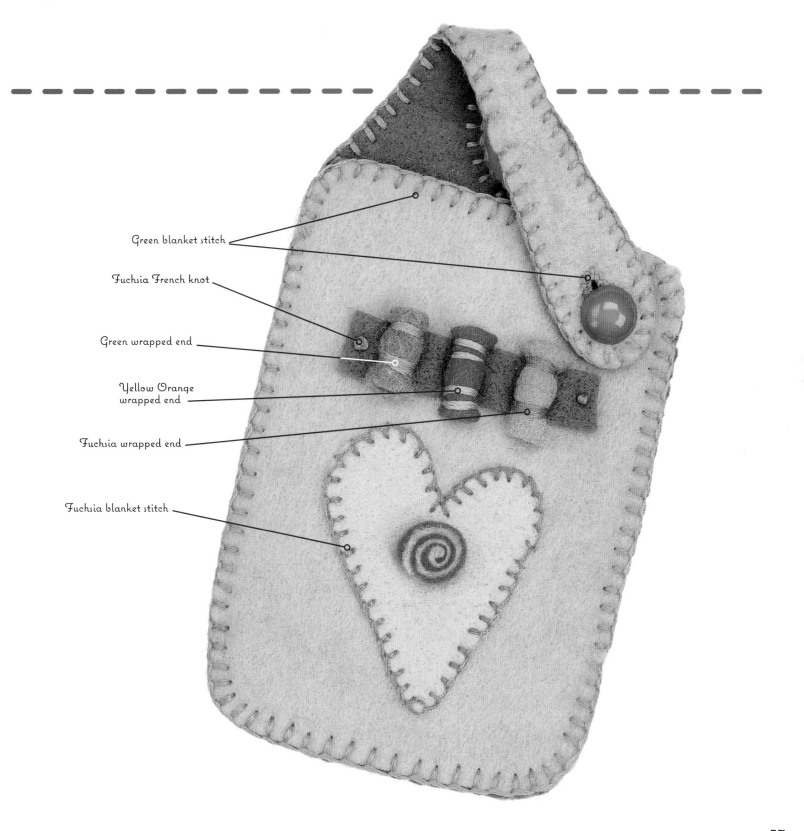

Green blanket stitch

Fuchsia French knot

Green wrapped end

Yellow Orange
wrapped end

Fuchsia wrapped end

Fuchsia blanket stitch

Starry Night Headband

Out for a night on the town? Make the
rounds while these flashy stars orbit your head.

What You Need

Felt

Red, 4 x 23 (10.2 x 58.4 cm)

Black, 4 x 23 inches (10.2 x 58.4 cm)

Decorative Thread

DMC embroidery floss, one skein each

Turquoise (#3844)

Light Lavender (#210)

Orange (#970)

Pink (#602)

Dark Fuchsia (#3804)

Bright Green (#907)

Gold (#728)

Blue Purple (#3746)

Black (#310)

Other Supplies

Small, sharp scissors

Black elastic, 3 x 1 inch (7.6 x 2.5 cm)

Basting spray

Sewing needle and thread (optional)

Sewing machine (optional)

What You Do

1 Transfer the headband pattern on pages 128–129; use the outside line for the red felt and the inside line for the black felt. Cut them out. Copy the stitch designs from the project photo onto the black felt. The circles do not have to be in the same exact locations. Carefully cut out the circles along the markings.

2 Add stitching around the circles as instructed in the following steps, but don't stitch the blanket stitches until you've joined the two headband pieces. Refer to the stitch instructions in the project photos.

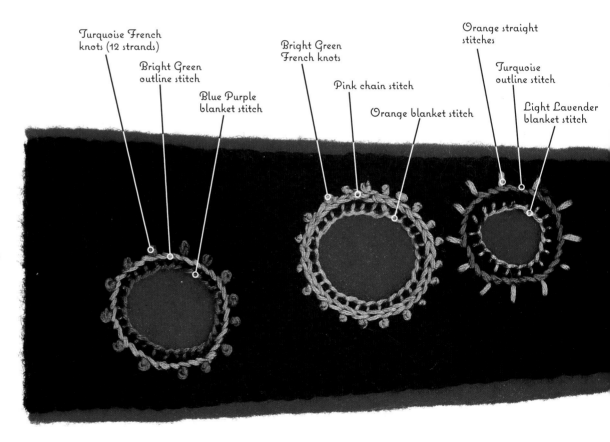

Turquoise French knots (12 strands)

Bright Green outline stitch

Blue Purple blanket stitch

Bright Green French knots

Pink chain stitch

Orange blanket stitch

Orange straight stitches

Turquoise outline stitch

Light Lavender blanket stitch

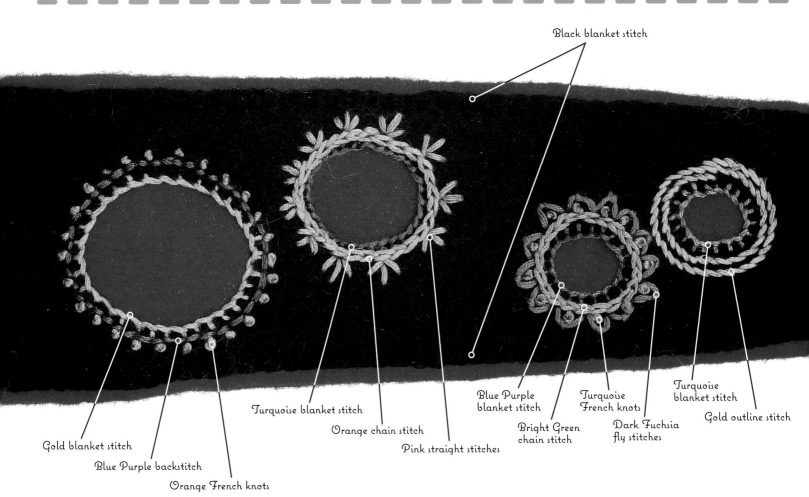

Black blanket stitch

Gold blanket stitch

Blue Purple backstitch

Orange French knots

Turquoise blanket stitch

Orange chain stitch

Pink straight stitches

Blue Purple blanket stitch

Bright Green chain stitch

Turquoise French knots

Dark Fuchsia fly stitches

Turquoise blanket stitch

Gold outline stitch

3 Start with the starburst design at the right end of the photo on page 59 and follow the stitches for the first three circles.

4 Flip around the headband and continue from left to right with the last four circles, as shown above. Then center the embroidered black felt piece over the red piece and blanket stitch them together. Blanket stitch inside each circle to attach the two pieces.

5 Using an embroidery needle or a sewing machine, attach one end of the elastic to one end of the headband. Try the headband on and pin the elastic to the opposite end to make it fit comfortably. Take the headband off and sew the elastic in place either by hand or by machine.

Hugs and Kisses Appliqués

Seal your things with
a kiss (and a hug)
with these appliqués!

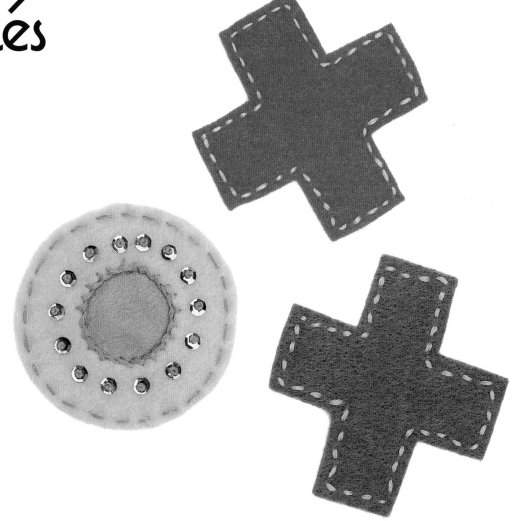

What You Need

Felt

Fuchsia, 4 x 4 inches (10.2 x 10.2 cm)

Lime green, 4 x 4 inches (10.2 x 10.2 cm)

Purple, 4 x 4 inches (10.2 x 10.2 cm)

Orange, 2 x 2 inches (5.1 x 5.1 cm)

Decorative Thread

DMC embroidery floss, one skein each

Lime Green (#3819)

Turquoise (#3845)

Pink (#602)

Other Supplies

14 bright pink sequins

Sewing needle and thread (optional)

Sewing machine (optional)

What You Do

1 Transfer the shapes onto the felt using the patterns on page 129 and cut them out.

2 Attach the sequins evenly around the lime green "O" with Turquoise French knots. Attach the orange circle to the middle of the "O" with a Turquoise blanket stitch.

3 Attach the appliqués in one of two ways:

Method 1: Attach the appliqués directly to the background item with running stitches as follows: the fuchsia "X" with the Pink floss, the lime green "O" with the Turquoise floss, and the purple "X" with the Lime Green floss.

Method 2: Embroider the perimeter of the appliqués with running stitches as above. Then, with matching sewing thread, hand slipstitch or machine-stitch them in place.

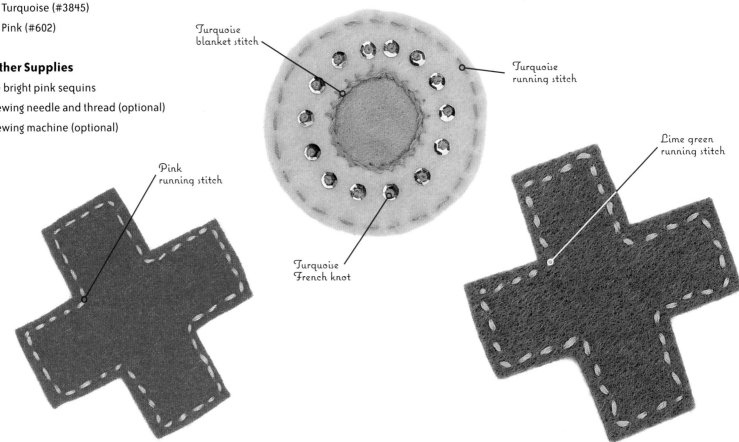

Pink running stitch

Turquoise blanket stitch

Turquoise running stitch

Turquoise French knot

Lime green running stitch

Floral Whimsy Purse

Sparkling sequins surround a delightful flower to brighten your day. A tassel adds to the fun.

Flower sequin
and gold bead

Other Supplies

Fabric glue

Sewing machine

Sewing thread in invisible, purple, and orange,
or matching bead colors

Straight pins

Sewing needle

Lightweight cardboard, 3 x 3¼ inch (7.6 x 8.3 cm)

What You Do

1 Make the stitch pattern on page 123 the
desired size, and cut out two pieces of
purple felt and two pieces of orange felt large
enough to hold the pattern. Transfer the stitch
pattern to one piece of the purple felt.

2 Stitch the design according to the
project photo.

3 Refer to Constructing a Purse on page
14 for detailed instructions for cutting,
assembling, and finishing the purse. Use matching color floss and thread. Add the beads and
sequins as shown in the project photo.

4 Make a 3¼-inch (8.3 cm) tassel (page 17)
with Purple and Orange yarn or floss for
the tassel and Black yarn or floss to wrap the
neck. Use Purple yarn or floss as the hanging
cord and to attach the tassel to the purse strap.
Thread the green bead first, and then the purple
and red beads, on the hanging cord before
securing it to the strap.

What You Need

Felt

Purple, ¾ yard (68.6 cm)

Orange, ¾ yard (68.6 cm)

Decorative Thread

Paternayan yarn or DMC embroidery floss

Paternayan yarn

Yellow (#772), 1 yard (91.4 cm)

Light Orange (#814), 4 yards (3.7 m)

Black (#220), 1 yard (91.4 cm)

Green (#669), 1 yard (91.4 cm)

Red (#97), 1 yard (91.4 cm)

DMC embroidery floss

Yellow (#743), 1 yard (91.4 cm)

Light Orange (#742), 4 yards (3.7 m)

Black (#310), 1 yard (91.4 cm)

Green (#701), 1 yard (91.4 cm)

Red (#817), 1 yard (91.4 cm)

Beads and Jewels

5 red flat-backed jewels, 4–5 mm

Pink flat-backed jewel, 7–8 mm

Package of multicolor flower sequins

Large green bead

Purple pony bead, ¼ inch (6 mm)

Red pony bead, ¼ inch (6 mm)

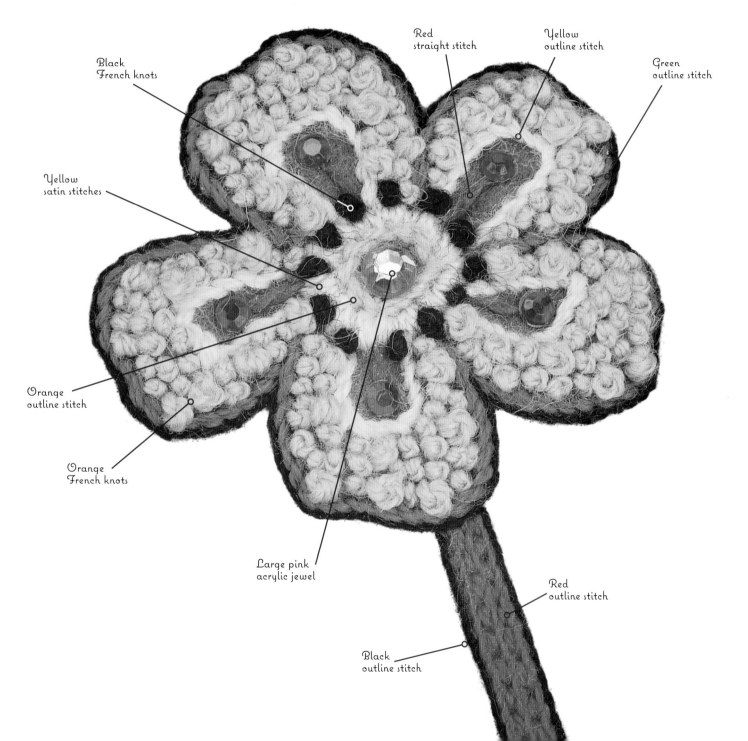

Black
French knots

Red
straight stitch

Yellow
outline stitch

Green
outline stitch

Yellow
satin stitches

Orange
outline stitch

Orange
French knots

Large pink
acrylic jewel

Red
outline stitch

Black
outline stitch

65

Natural Setting

The heart-shaped leaves and natural colors of this placemat-and-napkin-ring set will add ambiance to your table.

Cream blanket stitch

Sage Green blanket stitch

What You Need

Placemat
Felt
Cream, 14 x 22 inches (35.6 x 55.9 cm)

Sage, 13 x 17 inches (33 x 43.2 cm)

Dark sage, 3 x 12 inches (7.6 x 30.5 cm)

Napkin Ring
Felt
Cream, 6 x 6 inches (15.2 x 15.2 cm)

Dark sage, 3 x 3 inches (7.6 x 7.6 cm)

Decorative Thread
Paternayan yarn or DMC embroidery floss

> *Paternayan yarn, 1 yard (91.4 cm) each*
> Cream (#261)
> Sage Green (#653)
> Medium Green (#652)
> Dark Green (#650)
>
> *DMC embroidery floss, 1 skein each*
> Cream (#712)
> Sage Green (#3348)
> Medium Green (#471)
> Dark Green (#936)

Other Supplies
Rotary cutter and cutting mat (optional)

Small, sharp scissors

Basting spray

Straight pins

What You Do

Placemat Instructions

1 Cut a piece of cream felt 14 x 18 inches (35.6 x 45.7 cm). Transfer the heart-shaped leaf pattern (page 116) onto the remaining cream felt 13 times. Cut out all 13 cream heart-shaped leaves.

2 Copy the stems and small leaves from the project photo onto the dark sage felt piece. You don't need to copy the straight stitches, French knots, or the heart-shaped leaves. Make a placement marking for each heart-shaped leaf instead.

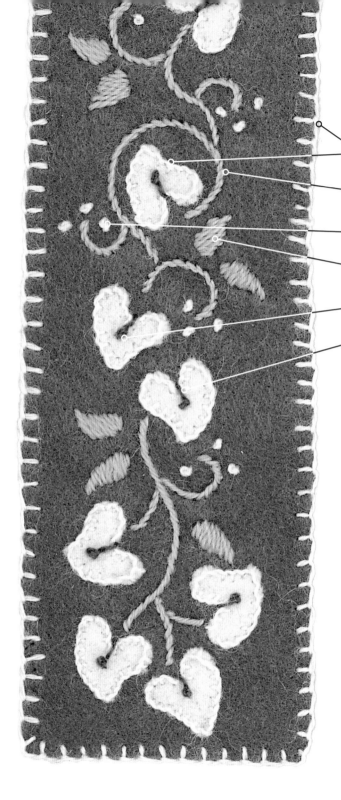

Cream blanket stitch

Sage Green outline stitch

Cream French knots

Sage Green satin stitch

Dark Green French knot

Dark Green straight stitch

3 Place the cream leaves on the marked felt. Stitch them according to the project photo.

4 Outline stitch all the stems and satin stitch the remaining leaves with Sage yarn or floss. Finish with Cream French knots at the end of each stem. Refer to the project photo for placement.

5 Spray baste the wrong side of the dark sage felt to attach it to the lighter sage felt, ⅜ inch (1 cm) from the center of a short edge. Blanket stitch around the edges of the dark sage piece with Cream yarn or floss.

6 Spray baste the light sage felt onto the center of the cream felt and blanket stitch around the edges with Dark Green yarn or floss.

Napkin Ring Instructions

1 Cut two pieces of cream felt, each 2 ½ x 6 inches (6.4 x 15.2 cm). Copy the stems and small leaves from the project photo onto one of the felt pieces. You don't need to copy the French knots or the heart-shaped leaves. Make a placement marking for each heart-shaped leaf instead.

2 Transfer the heart-shaped leaf onto the dark sage felt four times and then cut them out.

3 Pin or use basting spray to hold the leaves on the cream felt (refer to the project photo for placement, color, and stitches).

4 Blanket stitch the short ends of both pieces of cream felt together with Cream yarn or floss. Pin the two pieces, with wrong sides together, to form the ring, aligning the seams. Blanket stitch around both edges with Dark Green yarn or floss.

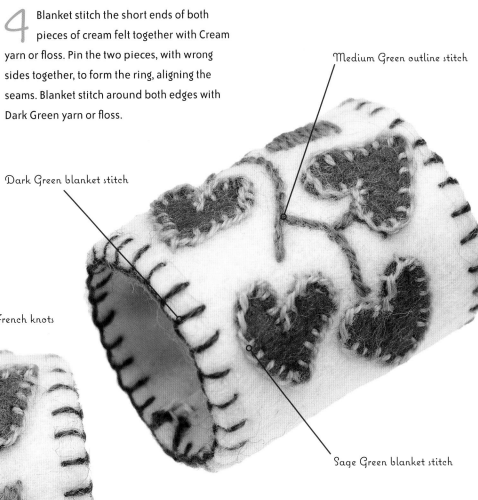

Medium Green outline stitch

Dark Green blanket stitch

Medium Green satin stitch

Sage Green French knots

Sage Green blanket stitch

Hungry Duckling Pincushion

This duck searches your sewing kit for scraps. Be careful where you stick those pins!

What You Need

Felt

Yellow, 8 x 8 inches (20.3 x 20.3 cm)

Orange, 4 x 4 inches (10.2 x 10.2 cm)

Yellow orange, 2 x 3 inches (5.1 x 7.6 cm)

Lime green, 2 x 4 inches (5.1 x 10.2 cm)

Pink (for base, color optional), 3 x 3 inches
   (7.6 x 7.6 cm)

Decorative Thread

DMC embroidery floss, one skein each

   Yellow (#742)

   Orange (#970)

   Purple (#3837)

   Fuchsia (#602)

   Black (#310)

Other Supplies

Sewing needle

Sewing thread in yellow, orange, and pink

Polyester fiberfill

Lightweight cardboard, 2 x 2 inches
   (5.1 x 5.1 cm)

Straight pins

Fabric glue

What You Do

1 Transfer the shapes onto the felt using the patterns on page 122 as follows: one yellow felt body, one orange felt bill, one orange felt pair of feet, and one yellow orange felt pair of feet. In addition, measure out one 3-inch (7.6 cm) diameter circle on the yellow felt. Cut out all the shapes. Copy the stitch designs onto the yellow body, following the project photo. Stitch the yellow wings.

2 Refer to Constructing a Pincushion on page 15 for further instructions. Use matching floss where appropriate. For the pincushion base, cut out a 1½-inch (3.8 cm) diameter circle from the lightweight cardboard. Cut out a 2½-inch (6.4 cm) diameter circle of pink felt.

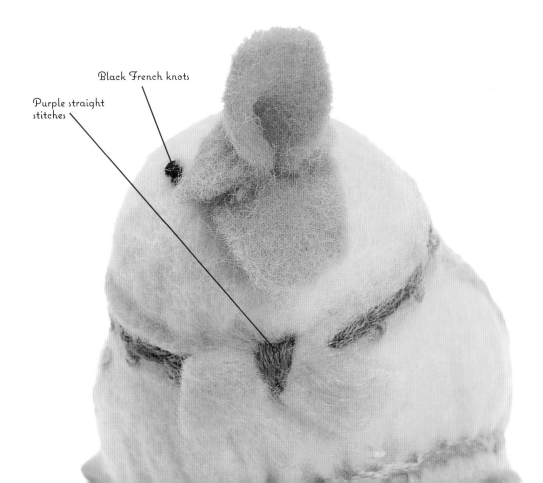

Black French knots

Purple straight stitches

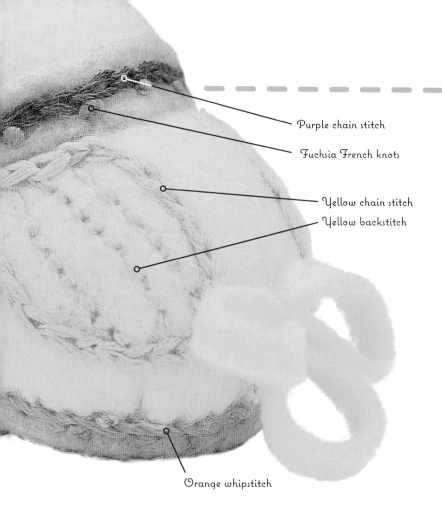

Purple chain stitch

Fuchsia French knots

Yellow chain stitch

Yellow backstitch

Orange whipstitch

7 Pin the head toward the front of the body, above the wings. Slipstitch or whipstitch it in place with yellow thread. Place the lime green collar around the neck, crossing it in front. Straight stitch over the crossed ends with Purple floss.

8 Dab a tiny bit of glue on the base of the duck bill and press it in place. Let the glue dry, and then secure the bill to the head with a slipstitch.

9 Stitch two French knots for eyes. Refer to the project photo for placement.

10 Cut three pieces of yellow felt, each $1/4 \times 3/4$ inch (6 x 19 mm). Run yellow thread or floss through each end of one strip to make a loop. Stitch the loop to the back of the duck at the tail (see the project photo for location). Repeat for the two remaining strips, sewing the loops close together.

3 Place the orange feet on top of the yellow orange feet. Stitch them together around the edges with an Orange running stitch.

4 Fold the duck bill in half and pinch the top half together. Sew a small straight stitch with orange thread to shape the bill (refer to the project photo).

5 Follow the stitch instructions for the collar (from the project photo) to stitch on the 2 x 4-inch (5.1 x 10.2 cm) piece of lime green felt. Trim the ends diagonally.

6 Slipstitch the feet, orange side up, under the base with the Orange floss.

Orange running stitch

Flower Power Hobo Bag

Bright and floral, this is
a little shoulder bag you
can take anywhere . . . even
back to Woodstock.

What You Need

Felt

Orange, 36 x 36 inches (91.4 x 91.4 cm)

Fuchsia, 36 x 36 inches (91.4 x 91.4 cm)

Pink, 6 x 6 inches (15.2 x 15.2 cm)

Lime green, 3 x 6 inches (7.6 x 15.2 cm)

Blue, 2 x 2 inches (5.1 x 5.1 cm)

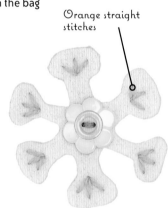

Decorative Thread

Paternayan yarn or DMC embroidery floss

Paternayan yarn, 1 yard (91.4 cm) each

Pink (#944)

Orange (#811)

Turquoise (#592)

Green (#698)

Yellow Orange (#813)

Dark Pink (#942)

DMC embroidery floss, one skein each

Pink (#604)

Orange (#970)

Turquoise (#3845)

Green (#907)

Yellow Orange (#972)

Dark Pink (#601)

Other Supplies

3 bright pink buttons, ½ inch (1.3 cm)
in diameter

2 yellow flower buttons, ¾ inch (1.9 cm)
in diameter

Sewing needle

Sewing thread, orange and fuchsia

Straight pins

Basting spray

Sewing machine (optional)

What You Do

1 Use hobo bag pattern on page 130 (at the correct size) to cut four pieces of the orange felt and four pieces of the fuchsia felt.

2 Transfer the shapes on page 125 to the felt. Refer to the project photo for placement.

3 Using the stitch instructions on the project photo as a guide, place the shapes on the bag with basting spray. Stitch them in place. Sew the buttons on last.

4 Use the instructions for Constructing a Hobo Bag on page 13 to finish the bag from the eight pieces of felt.

Orange French knots
(double-strand, around center)

Pink blanket stitch
(around edges)

Orange straight
stitches

Turquoise satin
stitch (to fill spokes)

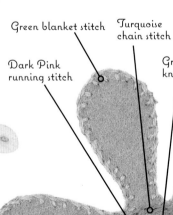

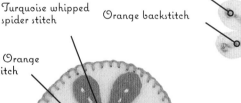

Yellow Orange
blanket stitch

Turquoise
running stitch

Yellow Orange
straight stitches

Green blanket stitch

Turquoise
chain stitch

Dark Pink
running stitch

Green French
knots (to fill)

Orange French knot

Orange backstitch

Turquoise whipped
spider stitch

Yellow Orange
chain stitch

Yellow Orange
running stitch

Turquoise blanket stitch

Fluffy Puppy Appliqué

Throw the dog a bone . . . or three. Here's a design that'll please all the dog lovers in your life.

Yellow Orange
blanket stitch

What You Need

Felt

Gold, 8 x 8 inches, (20.3 x 20.3 cm)

Cream, 4 x 4 inches (10.2 x 10.2 cm)

Dusty pink, 2 x 2 inches (5.1 x 5.1 cm)

Lavender, 1¼ x 5 inches (3.2 x 12.7 cm)

Periwinkle, 2 x 3 inches (5.1 x 7.6 cm)

Tan, 2 x 3 inches (5.1 x 7.6 cm)

Soft green, 2 x 3 inches (5.1 x 7.6 cm)

Decorative Thread

Paternayan yarn or DMC embroidery floss

Brown DMC floss (#975), one skein, when using either thread

Paternayan yarn, 1 yard (91.4 cm) each

Black (#220)

Fuchsia (#903)

Blue Lavender (#343)

Turquoise (#592)

Light Green (#663)

Yellow Orange (#813)

Orange (#811)

DMC embroidery floss, one skein each

Black (#310)

Fuchsia (#3804)

Blue Lavender (#156)

Turquoise (#3845)

Light Green (#907)

Yellow Orange (#742)

Orange (#740)

Other Supplies

Decorative flower button

Basting spray (optional)

Straight pins

What You Do

1 Transfer the shapes onto the felt using the patterns on page 122. Cut them out.

2 Stitch the collar according to the project photo for stitches and placement instructions.

3 Overlap the top of the collar and bottom of the head by ¼ inch (6 mm) and join the two pieces by blanket stitching with Light Green. See the project photo.

4 Attach the nose onto the muzzle with the Black thread or yarn, using the basting spray or pins. Backstitch the vertical line under and around the nose with the Black.

5 Pin the muzzle on the head with the tongue tucked underneath as shown in the photo. Follow the photo for stitches and colors. Do not stitch over the dog's tongue. Stitch the flower button to the collar, as shown in the project photo.

6 Blanket stitch the dog appliqué to the item with Blue Lavender thread. Use a Fuchsia blanket stitch to attach the soft green bone, a Light Green blanket stitch to attach the tan bone, and a Yellow Orange blanket stitch to attach the periwinkle bone.

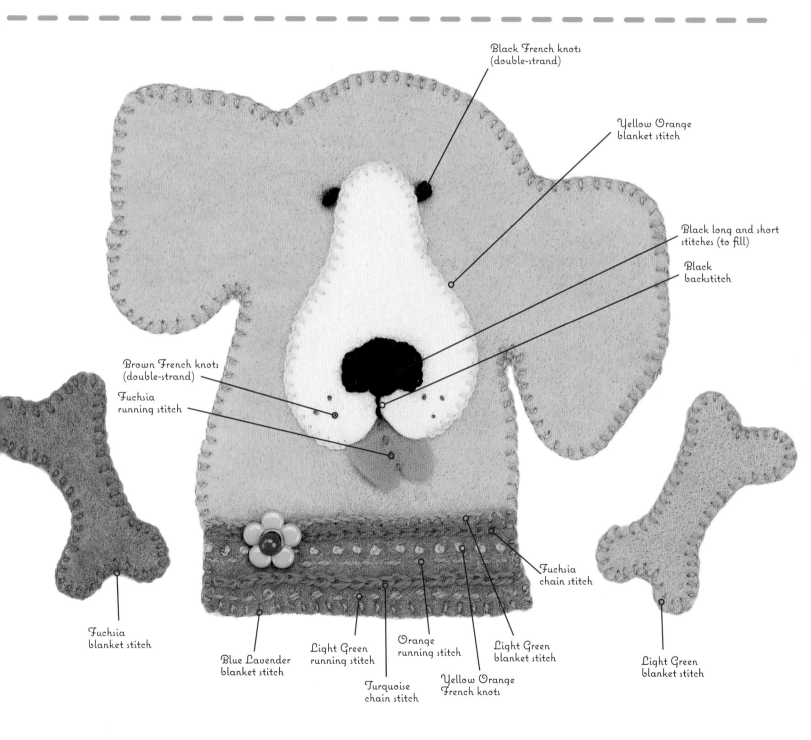

Black French knots
(double-strand)

Yellow Orange
blanket stitch

Black long and short
stitches (to fill)

Black
backstitch

Brown French knots
(double-strand)

Fuchsia
running stitch

Fuchsia
chain stitch

Fuchsia
blanket stitch

Blue Lavender
blanket stitch

Light Green
running stitch

Orange
running stitch

Light Green
blanket stitch

Light Green
blanket stitch

Turquoise
chain stitch

Yellow Orange
French knots

Starburst Bracelet

Bright colors on a black background highlight the starry stitches on your wrist.

What You Need

Felt
Black, 2 x 12 inches (5.1 x 30.5 cm)

Decorative Thread

DMC embroidery floss, 1 yard (91.4 cm) each
Pink (#961)
Light Pink (#963)
Turquoise (#3845)
Medium Green (#704)
Gold (#3854)
Red (#666)
Dark Green (#700)

DMC embroidery floss, 2 yards (1.8 m) each
Lime Green (#3819)
Orange (#3340)
Fuchsia (#3607)
Purple (#3837)

Other Supplies

Strip of 14-count plastic canvas, 12 x 1 inch (30.5 x 2.5 cm), or a piece of Buckram, 12 x 3 inches (30.5 x 7.6 cm)

Sewing needle

Sewing thread, invisible or black

4 flat-back acrylic jewels in purple, yellow, hot pink, and green

Fabric glue

Straight pins

What You Do

1 Measure your wrist and add 4 to 5 inches (10.2 to 12.7 cm) so the bracelet will slip over your hand. Cut the piece of 14-count plastic canvas or Buckram to this length. If you are using plastic canvas, overlap the short ends by 1 inch (2.5 cm) and stitch them firmly closed using floss or strong thread. If you are using Buckram, fold it in thirds lengthwise to provide more stiffness before overlapping and stitching. This piece should be able to slip over your hand. Set the piece aside.

2 Cut a piece of the black felt 2 inches (5.1 cm) wide by the length of the bracelet from step 1, plus ¼ inch (6 mm).

3 Copy the decorative stitching lines onto the felt from the project photo. The circles do not have to match exactly.

4 Refer to the stitch instructions in the project photo.

5 If the bracelet is so long there is an empty space at the ends, fill the space with Turquoise French knots (see the photo detail).

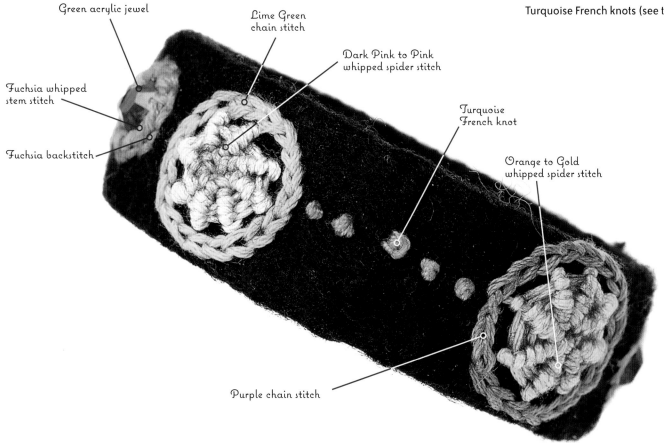

Green acrylic jewel

Lime Green chain stitch

Dark Pink to Pink whipped spider stitch

Fuchsia whipped stem stitch

Fuchsia backstitch

Turquoise French knot

Orange to Gold whipped spider stitch

Purple chain stitch

6 Glue the acrylic jewels in the centers of the small circles.

7 Center the embroidered felt, wrong side down, over the plastic bracelet and turn under one short end ⅛ inch (3 mm). Position the folded felt edge away from the overlapped plastic or Buckram ends to minimize bulk and slipstitch it to the bracelet with sewing thread.

8 Bring the other short end around to the folded, stitched-down edge. Fold this end under so that the felt is taut and slipstitch it down right next to the first folded edge.

9 Wrap the sides to the inside of the bracelet. Make sure the felt is taut; trim it if necessary to smooth the right side. Pin it down and slipstitch the edges together with matching sewing thread.

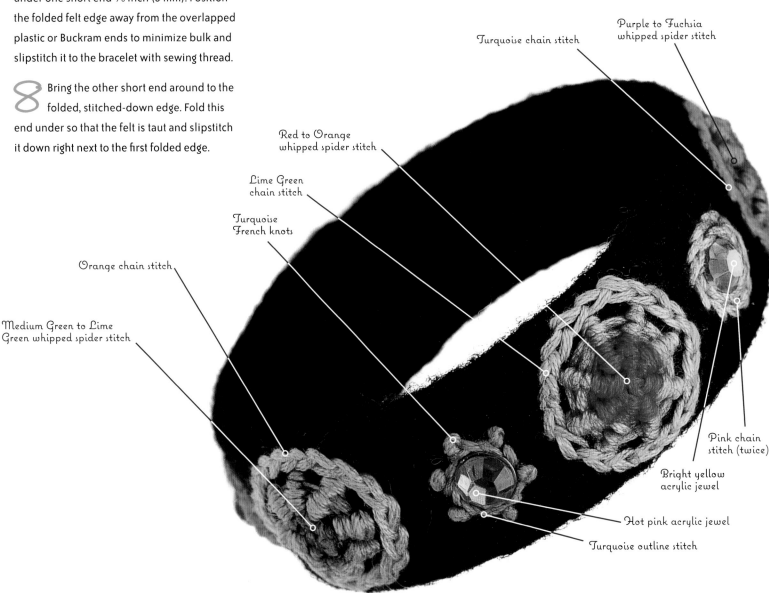

Turquoise chain stitch

Purple to Fuchsia whipped spider stitch

Red to Orange whipped spider stitch

Lime Green chain stitch

Turquoise French knots

Orange chain stitch

Medium Green to Lime Green whipped spider stitch

Pink chain stitch (twice)

Bright yellow acrylic jewel

Hot pink acrylic jewel

Turquoise outline stitch

Sweet Treat Pincushion

The cherry on top may look yummy, but don't eat it. It's for pins.

What You Need

Felt

Lime green, 4 x 6 inches (10.2 x 15.2 cm)

Red, 2 x 2 inches (5.1 x 5.1 cm)

Bright blue, 3 x 3 inches (7.6 x 7.6 cm)

Pale blue, 3 x 3 inches (7.6 x 7.6 cm)

Remnants for swirls, each 1 x 3 inches (2.5 x 7.6 cm), in bright blue, purple, green, pink, orange, fuchsia, and light green (or colors you have on hand)

Decorative Thread

DMC embroidery floss

    Blue Green (#958), 1 yard (91.4 cm)

    Brown (#420), 6 inches (15.2 cm)

Other Supplies

Lightweight cardboard, 2 x 2 inches

    (5.1 x 5.1 cm)

Sewing needle

Sewing thread in bright blue, lime green,

    and red

Polyester fiberfill

Fabric glue

What You Do

1 Measure and cut out the following circle patterns in the felt color indicated: a lime green 2½-inch (6.4 cm) diameter circle, a red 1 ¼-inch (3.2 cm) diameter circle, and a bright blue 2-inch (5.1 cm) diameter circle.

2 Transfer the scallop pattern on page 116 onto the bright blue felt and the pale blue felt. Cut them out. Blanket stitch the two scallop pieces together, around all the edges, with the Blue Green floss.

3 Cut out a 1¼-inch (3.2 cm) diameter circle from the lightweight cardboard for the pincushion base. Use the bright blue 2-inch (5.1 cm) felt circle for the base.

4 Refer to Constructing a Pincushion on page 15 for further instructions. Use matching floss where appropriate. Attach the cardboard base beneath the scalloped felt piece. Attach the body of the pincushion on top of the scalloped piece.

5 Thread the Brown floss through the center of the red felt circle. Trim the thread to 1½ inches (3.8 cm) and leave it loose on top of the circle.

6 Sew a red running stitch around the perimeter of the red circle, ⅛ inch (3 mm) from the outside edge. Leave the thread on the needle and pull it gently to gather the circle. Fill the circle with small bits of fiberfill until you have the shape and firmness you want. Pull the thread to create a cherry. Knot the thread.

7 Coat the brown floss with fabric glue and fold the end over ¼ inch (6 mm). Curve the floss slightly and hold it in place until it has stiffened. Slipstitch the cherry to the top of the pincushion with red thread or floss.

8 Make eight felt swirls in the following colors (or in any colors you have on hand): two green swirls with pink inside, two purple swirls with blue inside, two orange swirls with purple inside, and two fuchsia swirls with lime green inside. Cut felt strips for the swirls ¼ x 2½ inches (6 mm x 6.4 cm). See Making a Felt Swirl (page 16) for further instructions.

9 Apply glue to a flat side of each felt swirl and glue them to the lime green pincushion. Finger press the swirls together to fit.

Blue Green
blanket stitch

83

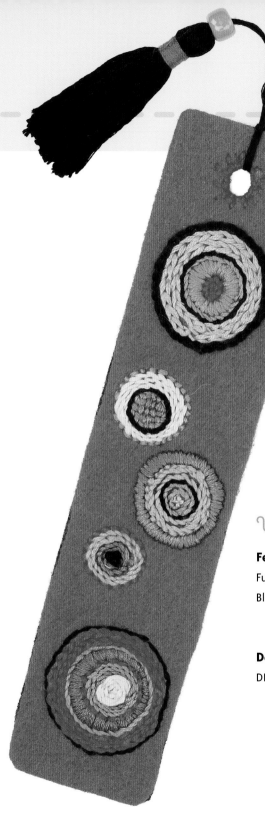

Bright Rings Bookmark

Cheerful circles hold your place.

Try the stitching as shown here or make

up your own patterns.

What You Need

Felt

Fuchsia, 1¾ x 7½ inches (4.5 x 19.1 cm)

Black, 1¾ x 7½ inches (4.5 x 19.1 cm)

Decorative Thread

DMC embroidery floss

Black (# 310), 5 yards (4.6 m)

Bright Pink (#957), 2 yards (1.8 m)

Green (#704), 1 yard (91.4 cm)

Yellow (#744), 1 yard (91.4 cm)

Yellow Orange (#740), 1 yard (91.4 cm)

Orange (#947), 2 yards (1.8 m)

Turquoise (#996), 2 yards (1.8 m)

Purple (#340), 2 yards (1.8 m)

Red (#606), 1 yard (91.4 cm)

Fuchsia (#3804), 1 yard (91.4 cm)

Other Supplies

Small, sharp scissors

Tapestry needle

Cardboard, 3 x 2¼ inches (7.6 x 5.7 cm)

Fabric glue or fusible web

Pink pony bead, ¼ inch (6 mm) in diameter

What You Do

1 Transfer the top, small circle of the pattern on page 118 onto the fuchsia and black felt pieces, which are already cut to bookmark size. Cut out the small circle at the top of each piece.

2 Refer to the project photo for stitch instructions and placement. The circles do not have to line up exactly with the bookmark in the photo.

3 Fuse or glue the wrong side of the embroidered fuchsia felt to the black felt. Align the top holes and blanket stitch through both holes with the Red floss.

4 Make the tassel (page 17) with the Black embroidery floss. Wrap the neck with the Fuchsia floss. Use a 3-inch (7.6 cm) length of Black floss for the hanging cord. Slide the pink pony bead onto the hanging cord and tie the ends of the tassel through the hole.

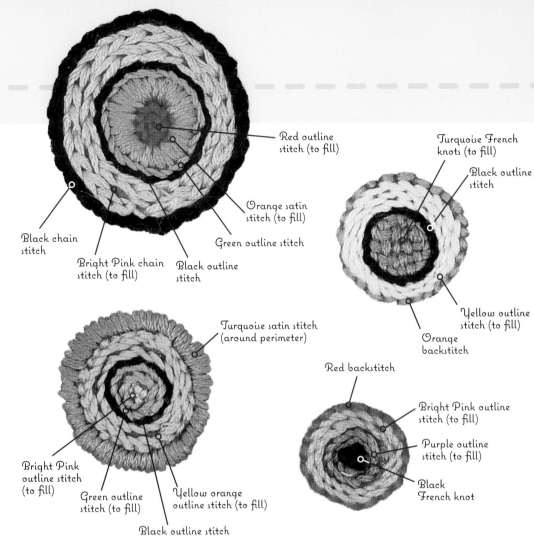

Black chain stitch

Bright Pink chain stitch (to fill)

Black outline stitch

Red outline stitch (to fill)

Green outline stitch

Orange satin stitch (to fill)

Turquoise French knots (to fill)

Black outline stitch

Orange backstitch

Yellow outline stitch (to fill)

Turquoise satin stitch (around perimeter)

Bright Pink outline stitch (to fill)

Green outline stitch (to fill)

Black outline stitch

Yellow orange outline stitch (to fill)

Red backstitch

Bright Pink outline stitch (to fill)

Purple outline stitch (to fill)

Black French knot

Black outline stitch

Red chain stitch (to fill)

Purple satin stitch (to fill)

Green outline stitch (to fill)

Turquoise outline stitch

Yellow whipped spider stitch

Orange outline stitch

Red outline stitch

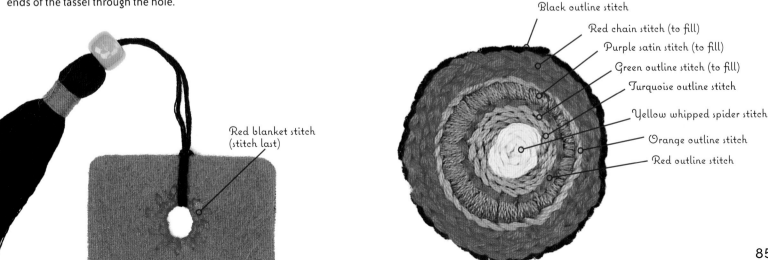

Red blanket stitch (stitch last)

85

Circle Game Pillow

Deck out this pillow top with circles of every stripe, swirl, and dot!

What You Need

Felt

Dark pink, 16 x 22 inches (40.6 x 55.9 cm)

Orange, 16 x 22 inches (40.6 x 55.9 cm)

Black, 22 x 22 inches (55.9 x 55.9 cm)

Lime green, 12 x 16 inches (30.5 x 40.6 cm)

Bright pink, 6 x 6 inches (15.2 x 15.2 cm)

Light pink, 6 x 6 inches (15.2 x 15.2 cm)

Decorative Thread

Paternayan yarn or DMC embroidery floss

Paternayan yarn

Pink (#944), 2½ yards (2.3 m)

Dark Pink (#943), 4½ yards (4.1 m)

Black (#220), 2½ yards (2.3 m)

Fuchsia (#903), 3½ yards (3.2 m)

Orange (#812), 3½ yards (3.2 m)

DMC embroidery floss

Pink (#3833), 2½ yards (2.3 m)

Dark Pink (#3932), 4½ yards (4.1 m)

Black (#310), 2½ yards (2.3 m)

Fuchsia (#600), 3½ yards (3.2 m)

Orange (#741), 3½ yards (3.2 m)

Other Supplies

Straight pins

Basting spray (optional)

Sewing needle

Sewing thread, invisible or matching felt

Sewing machine

Polyester fiberfill

What You Do

1 Cut a 16-inch (40.6 cm) square from both the dark pink and orange felt. Cut a 13 ½-inch (34.3 cm) square and a 7 ¼ x 6 ½-inch (18.4 x 16.5 cm) piece of black felt. Round the corners of the smaller black felt piece (refer to the project photo). Cut an 11-inch (27.9 cm) square of lime green felt. Save the remaining felt pieces for the appliqués.

2 Center and pin (or spray baste) the larger black square on top of the dark pink pillow top. Slipstitch it in place using black sewing thread. Center and pin (or spray baste) the lime green square on the black felt and slipstitch it in place using a matching sewing thread. Set aside the pillow top.

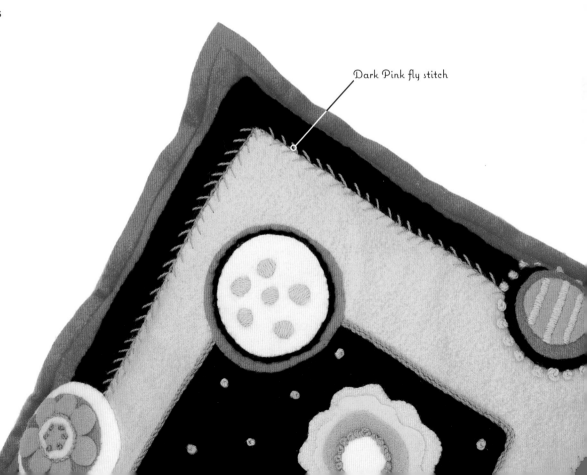

Dark Pink fly stitch

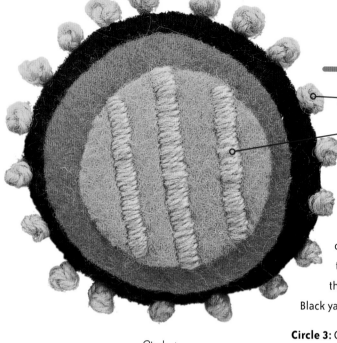

Orange French knots
Pink satin stitch

Circle 1

Circle 5: Cut the following shapes and stack them from largest to smallest: a large orange circle, a medium-size bright pink circle, and an extra-small lime green circle. Slipstitch the bright pink circle onto the orange circle. Copy the spiral design from the project photo onto the felt and satin stitch it with Fuchsia yarn or floss. Slipstitch the lime green circle in the center of the spiral.

of the dark pink circle and slipstitch them together. Chain stitch around the inner circle, using three strands of Black yarn or nine strands of Black floss.

Circle 3: Cut the following shapes and stack them from largest to smallest: a large bright pink scalloped circle, a smaller lime green scalloped circle, a small orange circle, and an extra small light pink circle. Slipstitch the layers together. Stitch Dark Pink French knots around the light pink circle, using three strands of yarn or nine strands of floss.

Circle 4: Cut the following shapes and stack them from largest to smallest: a large light pink circle, a small dark pink circle, an orange flower shape, and an extra-small bright pink circle. Slipstitch the layers together. Outline stitch through all layers around the bright pink circle with Dark Pink yarn or floss. Stitch six Fuchsia French knots, evenly spaced around the inner circle.

3 Make five felt circles using the circle patterns on page 123. Cut out the circles as indicated.

Circle 1: Cut three circles: a small orange circle, a medium pink circle, and a black large circle. Copy the stripe pattern from the project photo onto the orange circle. It doesn't have to match exactly. Satin stitch the stripes with Pink yarn or floss, working with one strand of yarn or three strands of floss for this project unless otherwise indicated. Layer the circles orange, pink, and black (from top to bottom). Slipstitch them together.

Circle 2: Cut two circles: a small light pink circle and a large dark pink circle. Copy the oval designs from the project photo onto the light pink circle and satin stitch them with Pink yarn or floss. Place the light pink circle on top

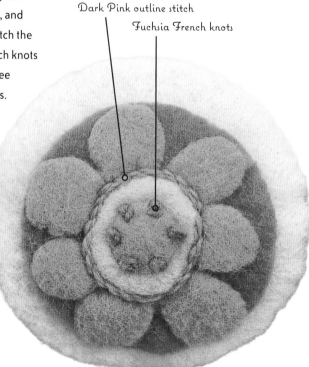

Dark Pink outline stitch
Fuchsia French knots

Circle 4

4 Pin Circle 3 to the smaller piece of black felt (see the project photo for placement) and slipstitch it in place. Copy the dot patterns onto the black felt or randomly stitch Pink or Orange French knots on the black felt, using three strands of yarn or nine strands of floss.

5 Pin and slipstitch the black felt piece and all the remaining circles to the lime green pillow top. Refer to the project photo for placement.

6 Outline stitch two Dark Pink rows around the black felt piece, stopping at the overlapping circles.

7 Stitch large, evenly spaced Orange French knots around Circle 1 with three strands of yarn or nine strands of floss.

8 Fly stitch a Dark Pink border around the lime green felt piece, stopping at the overlapping circles.

9 Pin the wrong side of the pillow top to the orange pillow back. Mark a stitching line ½ inch (1.3 cm) from all the sides. See Constructing a Basic Pillow (page 13) for finishing instructions.

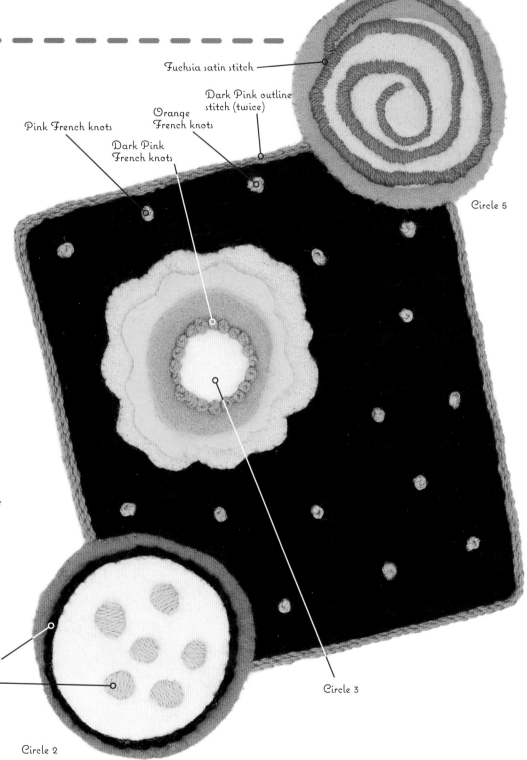

Fuchsia satin stitch

Dark Pink outline stitch (twice)

Orange French knots

Pink French knots

Dark Pink French knots

Circle 5

Black chain stitch

Pink satin stitch

Circle 2

Circle 3

89

Desert Sky Phone Carrier

No matter where you travel, your cell will always be right where you need it.

What You Need

Felt

Black, 10 x 12 inches (25.4 x 30.5 cm)

Red, 8 x 10 inches (20.3 x 25.4 cm)

Decorative Thread

DMC floss, one skein each

Red (#666)

Black (#310)

Purple (#3746)

Dark Gold (#782)

Gold (#3852)

Other Supplies

Hook-and-loop tape, 1 inch (2.5 cm) square

Sewing needle

Red and black sewing thread

Straight pins

Rounded black cord, ⅛ inch (3 mm) in width,
    1 yard (91.4 cm) long

What You Do

1 Transfer the shapes onto the felt using the patterns on page 124 as follows: one each of A, B, C, and F on the black felt; and two D shapes and one E on the red felt. Cut out the shapes. Refer to the project photo for the stitches you'll make on the F piece.

2 Using six strands of each floss for the embroidery, slipstitch one square of the hook-and-loop tape onto the center of one D felt piece with sewing thread (figure 1). Place the wrong sides of the two D pieces together and blanket stitch the top edges together with the Red floss (figure 1 again).

3 Place the F piece on the E near the curved top and embroider the two pieces together (figure 2).

4 Slipstitch the other piece of hook-and-loop tape near the top of piece A. Turn A over and pin piece E to it (figure 3). Blanket stitch the two pieces together with the Red floss.

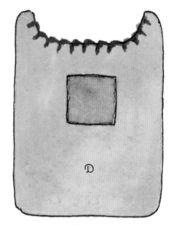

Figure 1

Figure 2

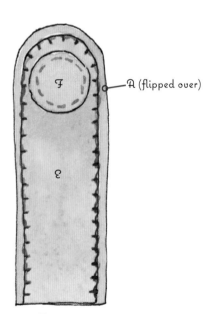

Figure 3

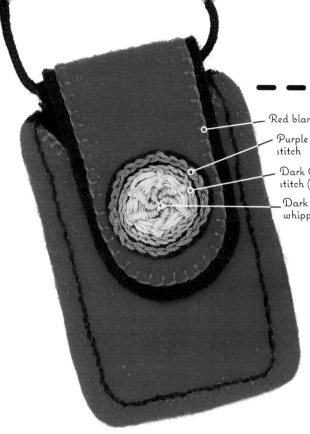

Red blanket stitch

Purple chain stitch

Dark Gold outline stitch (two rows)

Dark Gold to Gold whipped spider stitch

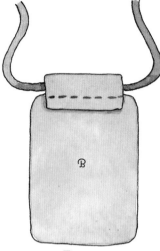

Figure 4

5 Place the ends of the cord just above the shaped section of piece B, and stitch the ends together. Fold the narrow top of piece B over the cord and backstitch it in place with the Black floss (figure 4).

6 Turn piece B over and pin piece A onto the back, 1 inch (2.5 cm) from the top edge. The hook-and-loop tape should be showing.

7 Pin piece C onto the back of piece B and backstitch the pieces together across the top, through all the layers (figure 5).

8 Center and pin the D pieces on top of piece B and—¼ inch (6 mm) from the sides and bottom edge—outline stitch them together with the Black floss (figure 6). Stitch through all the layers.

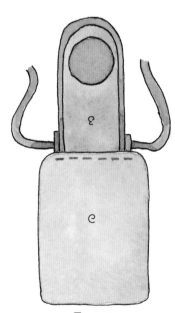

Figure 5

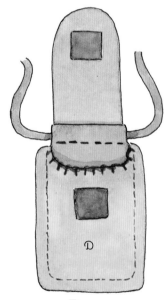

Figure 6

Belt of Many Paisleys

A felt belt? Once you make it, you won't want to take it off. The paisley designs add pizzazz.

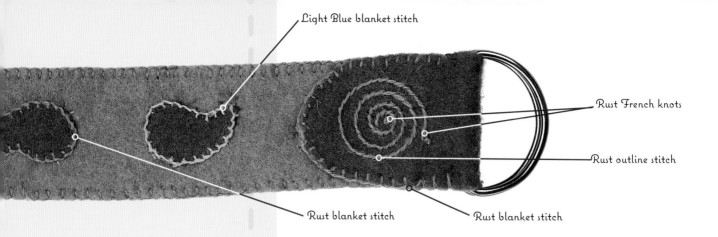

Light Blue blanket stitch

Rust French knots

Rust outline stitch

Rust blanket stitch

Rust blanket stitch

What You Need

Felt

Navy blue, 2 inches (5.1 cm) x waist measurement plus 6–8 inches (15.2–20.3 cm)

Rust, 2 inches (5.1 cm) x waist measurement plus 6–8 inches (15.2–20.3 cm)

Navy blue, 8 x 10 inches (20.3 x 25.4 cm) for appliqués

Decorative Thread

Paternayan yarn or DMC embroidery floss

Paternayan yarn
Light Blue (#504), 3 yards (2.7 m)
Navy (#501), 3 yards (2.7 m)
Rust (#403), 6 yards (5.5 m)

DMC embroidery floss
Light Blue (#3325), 1 skein
Navy (#312), 1 skein
Rust (#403), 2 skeins

Other Supplies

Small, sharp scissors

Basting spray

Straight pins

Antique bronze D rings, 2 inches (5.1 cm) in diameter

What You Do

1 Cut two pieces of navy blue and rust felt, each 2 inches (5.1 cm) wide by your waist measurement plus 6 to 8 inches (15.2 to 20.3 cm) long for overlap. For example, if your waist measures 30 inches, you might cut the felt 2 x 36 inches (5.1 x 91.4 cm).

2 Copy the swirl design from the project photo onto one end (now the top) of the blue felt piece and then transfer the paisley shape on page 116 repeatedly and evenly spaced from the top of the belt to the bottom. Cut out the paisley shapes with the small, sharp scissors.

3 Outline stitch around the swirl design and add French knots at the beginning and end with Rust yarn or floss. Refer to the project photo.

4 Spray baste the wrong side of the navy piece to the rust piece. Blanket stitch around all the paisley-shaped openings, alternately using Light Blue and Navy yarn or floss to attach them. Starting at the second paisley shape, stitch around the opening with a Rust running stitch. Skip one paisley-shaped opening

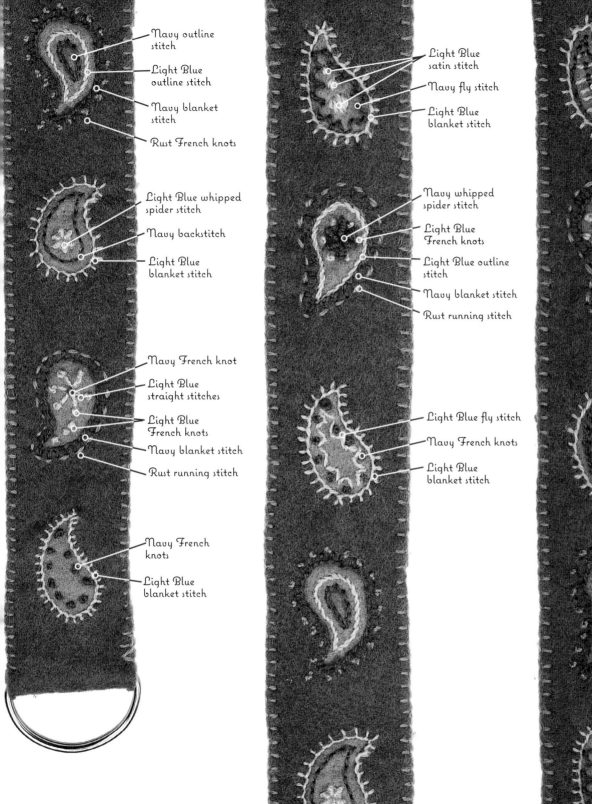

Navy outline stitch

Light Blue outline stitch

Navy blanket stitch

Rust French knots

Light Blue satin stitch

Navy fly stitch

Light Blue blanket stitch

Light Blue straight stitches

Navy straight stitches

Navy backstitch

Light Blue blanket stitch

Light Blue whipped spider stitch

Navy backstitch

Light Blue blanket stitch

Navy whipped spider stitch

Light Blue French knots

Light Blue outline stitch

Navy blanket stitch

Rust running stitch

Navy outline stitch

Light Blue French knots

Navy blanket stitch

Rust running stitch

Navy French knot

Light Blue straight stitches

Light Blue French knots

Navy blanket stitch

Rust running stitch

Light Blue fly stitch

Navy French knots

Light Blue blanket stitch

Light Blue seed stitches

Navy chain stitch

Light Blue blanket stitch

Navy French knots

Light Blue blanket stitch

Navy lazy daisy "leaves"

Navy outline stitch

Light Blue running stitch

Navy blanket stitch

Rust French knots

and stitch around the fourth opening with Rust French knots. Repeat this pattern (running stitch, no additional stitching, French knots) for the length of the belt.

5 Insert the top of the belt through the D ring and fold it over. Pin it in place so that the swirl is on the inside (or back) of the belt. Starting next to the D rings, blanket stitch around the belt, through all the layers, with Rust yarn or floss. Go back, and blanket stitch the loose, swirl-end of the belt down to the rust felt with the same yarn or floss.

6 Copy the decorative stitch patterns from the project photo to add the decorative stitches inside the paisley-shaped cutouts.

7 Transfer the paisley shape design onto the remaining blue felt enough times so that you have the same number of blue paisleys as there are paisley cutouts on the belt. Blanket stitch the blue cutouts onto the rust side of the belt, directly behind the cutouts to cover the stitching. Stitch only through the rust layer of felt, alternately using Light Blue and Rust yarn or floss.

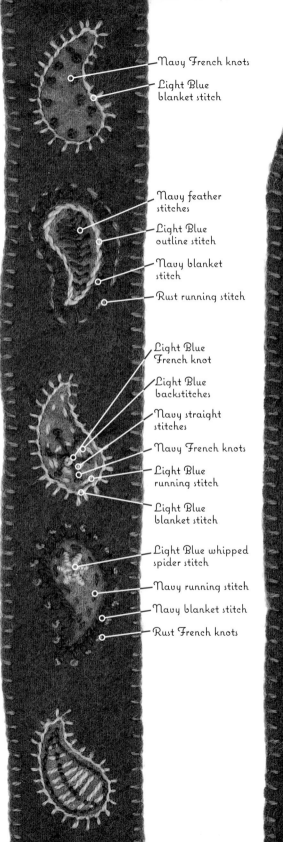

Navy French knots
Light Blue blanket stitch
Navy feather stitches
Light Blue outline stitch
Navy blanket stitch
Rust running stitch
Light Blue French knot
Light Blue backstitches
Navy straight stitches
Navy French knots
Light Blue running stitch
Light Blue blanket stitch
Light Blue whipped spider stitch
Navy running stitch
Navy blanket stitch
Rust French knots

Navy whipped spider stitch
Light Blue outline stitch
Navy blanket stitch
Rust French kn
Navy satin stit
Light Blue blanket stitch
Navy outline stitch
Light Blue French knots
Navy blanket stitch
Rust running sti
Light Blue straight stitche
Navy chain st
Light Blue blanket stitch
Navy straight stitches
Navy running stitch
Light Blue fly stitch
Navy blanket stitch
Rust French kn

Bee Colorful Pincushion

Your pins will always bee where you left
them: in this multi-colored bumble.

What You Need

Felt

Orange, 4 x 4 inches (10.2 x 10.2 cm)

Turquoise, 3 x 3 inches (7.6 x 7.6 cm)

Fuchsia, 3 x 4 inches (7.6 x 10.2 cm)

Yellow orange, 3 x 3 inches (7.6 x 7.6 cm)

Yellow, 1½ x 1½ inches (3.8 x 3.8 cm)

Pink, 2 x 2 inches (5.1 x 5.1 cm)

Lime green, scrap

Decorative Thread

DMC embroidery floss, 1 yard (91.4 cm) each

    Pink (#603)

    Blue Lavender (#155)

    Blue (#996)

    Black (#301)

Other Supplies

Sewing needle

Sewing thread, matching felt colors

Polyester fiberfill

Lightweight cardboard, 1½ x 1½ inches
   (3.8 x 3.8 cm)

Fabric glue

Straight pins

2 quilter's straight pins with yellow heads

What You Do

1. Transfer the shapes onto the felt using the patterns on page 118 and cut them out.

2. Place the two wings together and blanket stitch around the edges with the Pink floss.

3. Refer to the project photo to embroider the bee body.

4. Cut out a 1¼-inch (3.2 cm) circle from the lightweight cardboard for the pincushion base. Cut out a 1¾-inch (4.5 cm) circle of pink felt for the base pattern.

5. Refer to Constructing a Pincushion on page 15 for further instructions. Use matching floss where appropriate.

6. Embroider four French knots with twelve strands of Black floss on each side of the body near the base to simulate feet. Refer to the project photo for placement.

7. Pin the wings onto the back of the bee (see the project photo for the wing location) with the fuchsia side up. Stitch the base of the wings to the body so that the wing tips remain loose. Cut a 1-inch (2.5 cm) diameter circle of yellow felt and pin it at the neck, covering the base of the wings. Whipstitch the circle onto the body. Pin the head over the yellow felt circle and slipstitch it in place with matching thread.

8. Cut a length of the Black floss and tie a knot. Hide the knot between the body and yellow neck circle. Wrap the floss around the neck two or three times above and below the circle of yellow felt. Hide the finishing knot.

9. Cut four pieces of felt, two each of fuchsia and lime green, 1½ x ⅛ inches (3.8 cm x 3 mm). Apply glue to one side of the fuchsia piece and place the lime green piece on top. Repeat. Roll up each stack of felt to create the eyes. Stitch a French knot in the center of each eye with the Black floss. Glue the eyes onto the head, referring to the project photo for placement.

Black French knot

10 To make the antennae, bend one quilter's straight pin about 3/8 inch (1 cm) from the top at a 45° angle. Coat an 8-inch (20.3 cm) length of Black floss with glue and wrap it around the pin starting just under its head. Smooth the floss so it completely covers the pin surface. Let the floss dry. Lightly coat the unwrapped part of the pin with the glue and insert it into the head of the bee. Repeat to create the other antenna.

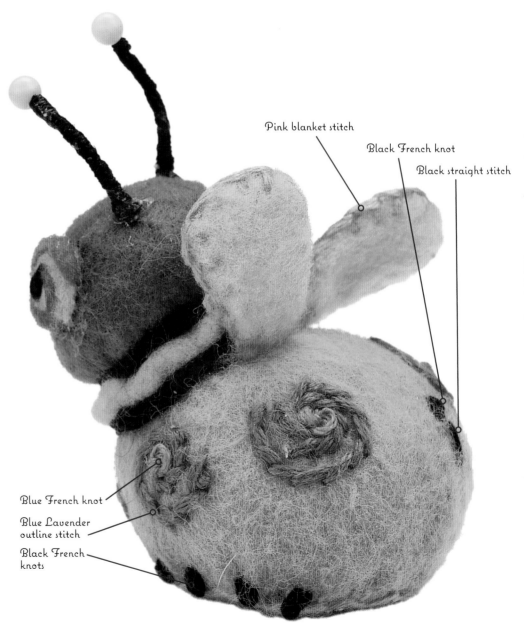

Pink blanket stitch

Black French knot

Black straight stitch

Blue French knot

Blue Lavender outline stitch

Black French knots

Summer's End Pillow

Combining the beauty of spring with the colors of autumn, this pillow fits every season.

What You Need

Felt

Orange, 20 x 20 inches (50.8 x 50.8 cm)

Fuchsia, 10 x 15 inches (25.4 x 38.1 cm)

Green, 15 x 20 inches (38.1 x 50.8 cm)

Yellow, 8 x 8 inches (20.3 x 20.3 cm)

Decorative Thread

Paternayan yarn or DMC embroidery floss

Paternayan yarn

Orange (#811), 6 yards (5.5 m)

Green (#699), 2 yards (1.8 m)

Light Green (#698), 3 yards (2.7 m)

Purple (#301), 2 yards (1.8 m)

Pink (#943), 1 yard (91.4 cm)

Red (#970), 1 yard (91.4 cm)

DMC embroidery floss

Orange (#970), 6 yards (5.5 m)

Green (#700), 2 yards (1.8 m)

Light Green (#704), 3 yards (2.7 m)

Purple (#3871), 2 yards (1.8 m)

Pink (#335), 1 yard (91.4 cm)

Red (#321), 1 yard (91.4 cm)

Other Supplies

Sewing needle

Sewing thread, invisible or matching felt
   or beads

Straight pins

7 turquoise 5-mm beads

5 light green 5-mm beads

Basting spray (optional)

Sewing machine

Polyester fiberfill

What You Do

1 Cut the orange felt to 15 x 20 inches (38.1 x 50.8 cm). Transfer the flower and leaf shapes from page 117 to the felt. Cut them out. Refer to the project photo as needed.

2 Create the center of the flower using a whipped spider stitch. Complete the stitching according to the project photo.

3 Stitch the six Orange rays and fill in the band around the center. Refer to the project photo as needed. Backstitch the purple veins on the leaf.

4 Slipstitch the flower in place.

Pink whipped spider stitch

Red backstitch

Purple French knots (to fill)

Orange woven picot stitches

Turquoise beads

Light Green backstitch

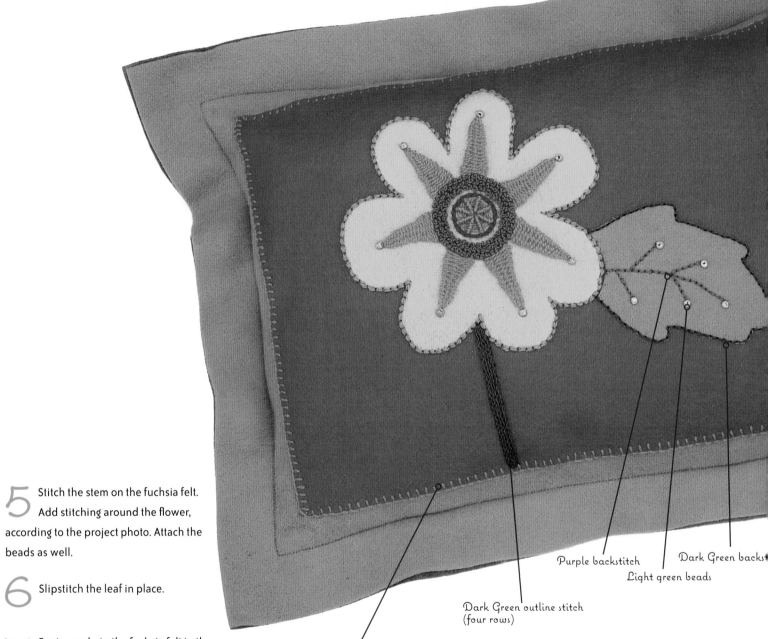

Purple backstitch

Dark Green backs*

Light green beads

Dark Green outline stitch
(four rows)

Orange blanket stitch

5 Stitch the stem on the fuchsia felt. Add stitching around the flower, according to the project photo. Attach the beads as well.

6 Slipstitch the leaf in place.

7 Center and pin the fuchsia felt to the orange felt. Blanket stitch them together.

8 Pin the wrong side of the orange pillow top to the green pillow back and mark a stitching line 1$\frac{1}{2}$ inch (3.8 cm) from all the sides. See Constructing a Basic Pillow (page 13) for finishing instructions.

May Flowers Purse

April showers have come and gone; butterflies and blossoms color the world. Celebrate spring!

What You Need

Felt

Fuchsia, each ³⁄₄ yard (68.6 cm)
Green, each ³⁄₄ yard (68.6 cm)

Decorative Thread

Paternayan yarn or DMC embroidery floss

Paternayan yarn
Yellow (#772), 1 yard (91.4 cm)
Light Orange (#814), 2 yards (1.8 m)
Orange (#813), 1 yard (91.4 cm)
Black (#220), 1 yard (91.4 cm)
Green (#669), 4 yards (3.7 m)
Turquoise (#592), 3 yards (2.7 m)

DMC embroidery floss
Yellow (#743), 1 yard (91.4 cm)
Light Orange (#742), 2 yards (1.8 m)
Orange (#741), 1 yard (91.4 cm)
Black (#310), 1 yard (91.4 cm)
Green (#701), 4 yards (3.7 m)
Turquoise (#3845), 3 yards (2.7 m)

Beads

5 black 2-mm seed beads
22 gold 3-mm beads
12 green 3-mm beads
40 turquoise 2-mm seed beads
Silver decorative bead, ¹⁄₂ inch (1.3 cm)
    in diameter
Orange pony bead, ¹⁄₄ inch (6 mm)
Green pony bead, ¹⁄₄ inch (6 mm)

Other Supplies

Sewing thread, fuchsia and green, or invisible
Sewing machine
Straight pins
Sewing needle
Lightweight cardboard, 3 x 3¹⁄₄ inch (7.6 x 8.3 cm)

What You Do

1 Make the stitch pattern on page 127 the desired size, and cut out two pieces of fuchsia felt and two pieces of green felt large enough to hold the pattern. Transfer the stitch pattern onto one piece of the fuchsia felt.

2 Stitch the design according to the project photo.

3 Refer to Constructing a Purse on page 14 for detailed instructions for cutting, assembling, and finishing the purse. Use matching color floss and thread. Add the beads as shown in the project photo.

4 Make a 3¹⁄₄-inch (8.3 cm) tassel (page 17) with Green yarn or floss for the tassel and Turquoise yarn or floss to wrap the neck. Use Turquoise yarn or floss as the hanging cord and to attach the tassel to the purse strap. Thread a silver bead and then the green and orange beads on the hanging cord before securing it to the strap.

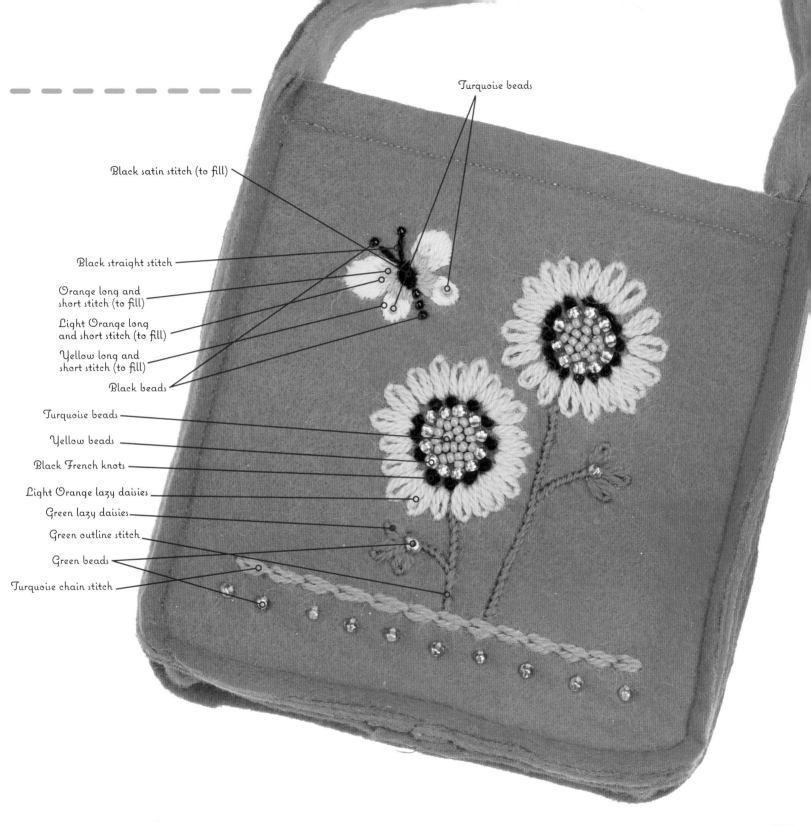

Turquoise beads

Black satin stitch (to fill)

Black straight stitch

Orange long and
short stitch (to fill)

Light Orange long
and short stitch (to fill)

Yellow long and
short stitch (to fill)

Black beads

Turquoise beads

Yellow beads

Black French knots

Light Orange lazy daisies

Green lazy daisies

Green outline stitch

Green beads

Turquoise chain stitch

Festival Felt Scarf

Felt is naturally warm—perfect for scarves. Here's one for any festive occasion.

What You Need

Felt

2 pieces of sage green, 4 x 72 inches (10.2 x 182.9 cm) and 8 x 8 inches (20.3 x 20.3 cm)

Cream, 4 x 8 inches (10.2 x 20.3 cm)

Blue lavender, 8 x 10 inches (20.3 x 25.4 cm)

Gold, 4 x 8 inches (10.2 x 20.3 cm)

Turquoise, 3 x 4 inches (7.6 x 10.2 cm)

Lavender, 4 x 72 inches (10.2 x 182.9 cm)

Note: If you can't find 72-inch (182.9 cm) lengths of felt, use two 36½-inch (92.7 cm) lengths and seam them together.

Decorative Thread

Paternayan yarn

    Blue Lavender (#343), 18 yards (16.5 m)

    Green (#613), 6 yards (5.5 m)

    Yellow Gold (#814), 3 yards (2.7 m)

    Magenta (#903), 3 yards (2.7 m)

    Turquoise (#592), 3 yards (2.7 m)

    Purple (#312), 3 yards (2.7 m)

    Orange (#813), 3 yards (2.7 m)

    Black (#220), 1 yard (91.4 cm)

Other Supplies

Sewing needle

Sewing thread, invisible

Magenta yarn, 18 inches (45.7 cm)

Fabric glue

Straight pins

Basting spray (optional)

Lightweight cardboard, 1½ x 3 inches
    (3.8 x 7.6 cm)

Strong thread or floss, 18 inches (45.7 cm)

Wire brush

What You Do

1 Transfer the patterns for the three squares on page 116 onto the cream felt and cut them out. Copy the swirl patterns onto the squares, according to the project photo.

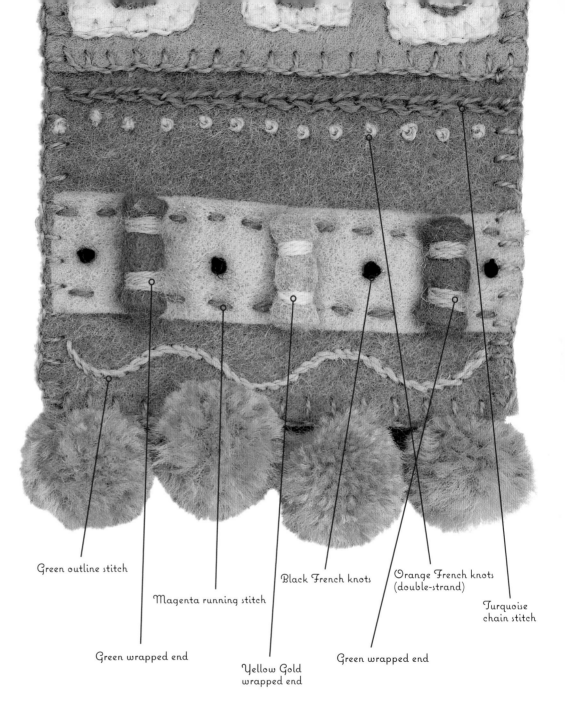

Green outline stitch

Magenta running stitch

Black French knots

Orange French knots
(double-strand)

Turquoise
chain stitch

Green wrapped end

Yellow Gold
wrapped end

Green wrapped end

2 Cut the remaining felt pieces by the following measurements:

Blue lavender: 1 x 4 inches (2.5 x 10.2 cm) and 2 x 4 inches (5.1 x 10.2 cm)

Cream: 2 x 4 inches (5.1 x 10.2 cm)

Gold: two pieces each 1 x 4 inches (2.5 x 10.2 cm)

Sage: $2\frac{1}{4}$ x 4 inches (5.7 x 10.2 cm)

3 Stitch the swirl patterns according to the project photo. Blanket stitch the cream squares onto the 2 x 4-inch (5.1 x 10.2 cm) sage green piece with Yellow Gold yarn.

4 Place the narrow green sage shape on the 2 x 4-inch (5.1 x 10.2 cm) blue lavender rectangle. Attach them according to the project photo.

5 Make the following felt rolls:

Cut a $1\frac{1}{2}$ x 3-inch (3.8 x 7.6 cm) piece of blue lavender felt. Cut three $3\frac{1}{2}$-inch (8.9 cm) lengths of Magenta yarn and lay them evenly together across one end of the felt. Use fabric glue to hold them in place, and then roll up the felt lengthwise around the yarn. Wrap each end of the roll with an Orange-Green-Orange yarn combination. Separate the yarn that hangs out of each end of the roll.

Cut two $\frac{3}{4}$ x 3-inch (1.9 x 7.6 cm) pieces of turquoise felt and roll each up separately. Wrap the ends with Green yarn.

Cut a $\frac{3}{4}$ x 3-inch (1.9 x 7.6 cm) piece of blue lavender felt and roll it up. Wrap the ends with Yellow Gold yarn.

6 Slipstitch the three small felt rolls evenly across a yellow gold strip.

7 Place the longer roll horizontally on a 1 x 4-inch (2.5 x 10.2 cm) strip of yellow gold felt. Slipstitch the roll in place from the back with invisible thread. Center the yellow gold felt on the 2 x 4-inch (5.1 x 10.2 cm) cream felt rectangle. Using Turquoise yarn, attach the yellow gold piece to the cream piece with a blanket stitch.

8 Pin all the felt shapes onto the long lavender scarf piece and attach them according to the project photo. Copy the wavy line from the photo to the bottom of the scarf and stitch it according to the photo detail.

9 Measure down from the green rectangle with the small cream squares $\frac{1}{4}$ inch (6 mm), and stitch the borders according to the project photo.

10 Measure down from the cream rectangle $\frac{1}{4}$-inch (6 mm) and stitch according to the project photo.

11 Measure down from the top blue lavender strip $\frac{1}{8}$-inch (3 mm) and stitch. Refer to the photo.

12 Repeat steps 1 to 11 on the right side of the other end of the scarf.

13 Pin or spray baste the wrong side of the stitched lavender felt to the green felt. Blanket stitch the pieces together around all the sides with Blue Lavender yarn. Stitch through all the layers of felt, including the appliqués.

14 Make eight pompoms, four from Blue Lavender yarn and four from Green. Cut a piece of cardboard $1\frac{1}{2}$ x 3 inches (3.8 x 7.6 cm). Wrap two 18-inch (45.7 cm) three-strand lengths of yarn around the cardboard. Carefully slip the yarn off the cardboard and tie the strands in the middle with an 18-inch (45.7 cm) length of strong thread or floss, leaving 6-inch (15.2 cm) lengths for attaching the pompom to the scarf. Brush the pompom with a wire brush to fluff it. Then trim it into a ball. Attach four pompoms in alternating colors to each end of the scarf.

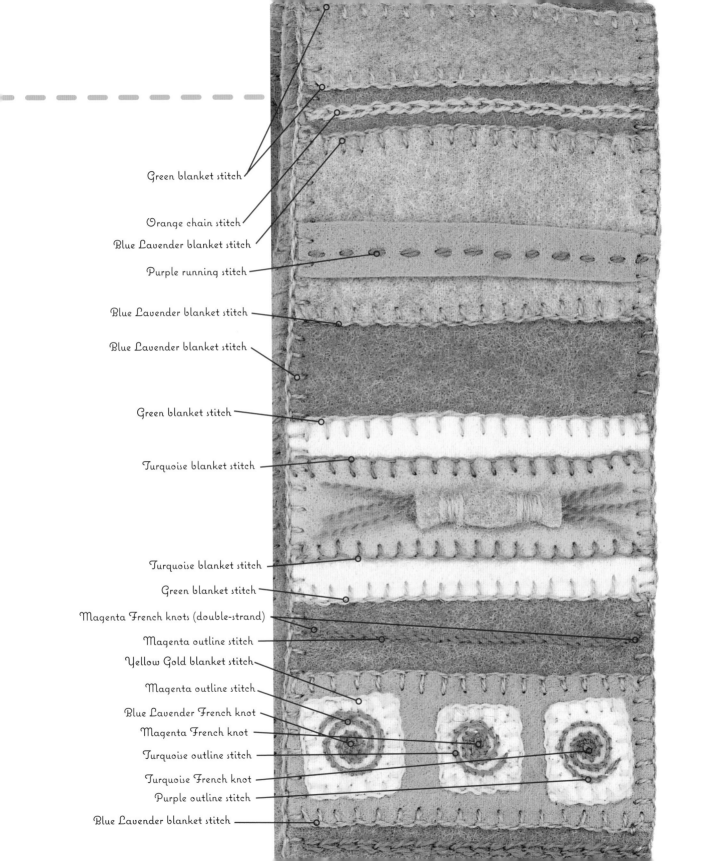

Green blanket stitch

Orange chain stitch

Blue Lavender blanket stitch

Purple running stitch

Blue Lavender blanket stitch

Blue Lavender blanket stitch

Green blanket stitch

Turquoise blanket stitch

Turquoise blanket stitch

Green blanket stitch

Magenta French knots (double-strand)

Magenta outline stitch

Yellow Gold blanket stitch

Magenta outline stitch

Blue Lavender French knot

Magenta French knot

Turquoise outline stitch

Turquoise French knot

Purple outline stitch

Blue Lavender blanket stitch

109

Embroidery Stitches

Don't know embroidery but you really want to do these fun projects? No problem. This little handy reference section shows you how simple these stitches really are. Whenever you come across a stitch you don't recognize, just slip back here and look it up. You'll be embroidering in no time!

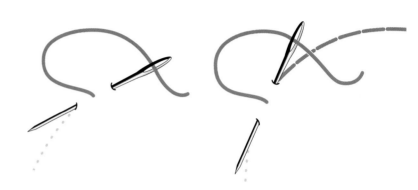

Backstitch

Backstitch

Space the stitches evenly to resemble a line of machine stitching.

Blanket Stitch

Vertical legs are always spaced apart. Work from left to right and end with a short tack stitch.

Chain Stitch

After forming a thread loop, snug up the loop against the working thread. Then form a second loop. Repeat.

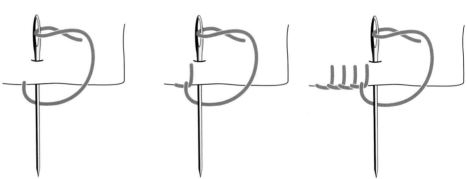

Blanket Stitch

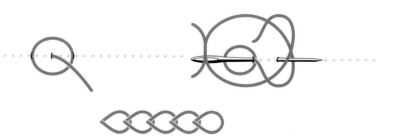

Chain Stitch

Feather Stitch

A decorative line stitch, this works well on straight or curved lines. Work from the top to the bottom.

Fishbone

Each time the needle returns to center, insert it slightly to the left or right of the central guide-line.

Fly Stitch

The length of the tie-down leg can be short or long to give different appearances.

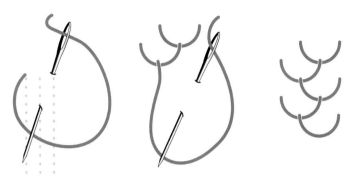

Feather Stitch

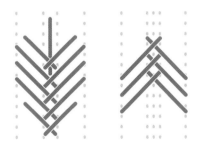

Fishbone

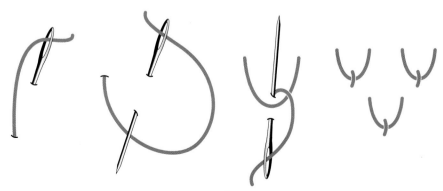

Fly Stitch

French Knot

Wrap the thread around the needle once or twice, and then insert it back into the fabric at point where the needle emerged.

Herringbone Stitch

Keep the spacing and length of stitches uniform. Keep similar angled legs parallel.

Lazy Daisy

This popular pattern is comprised of single Chain stitches.

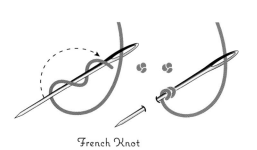

French Knot

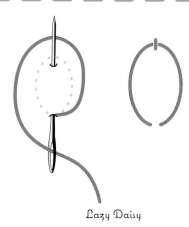

Lazy Daisy

Herringbone Stitch

Long and Short

The first row alternates long and short straight stitches. Successive rows have all the stitches same length as long stitches.

Outline Stitch

Work from left to right, keeping the stitches the same size.

Palestrina

A series of intricate knots that when finished create a line with a beaded look.

Running Stitch

All stitches are equal length, both on top and on the bottom of the fabric.

Satin Stitch

This stitch is composed of parallel rows of straight stitches.

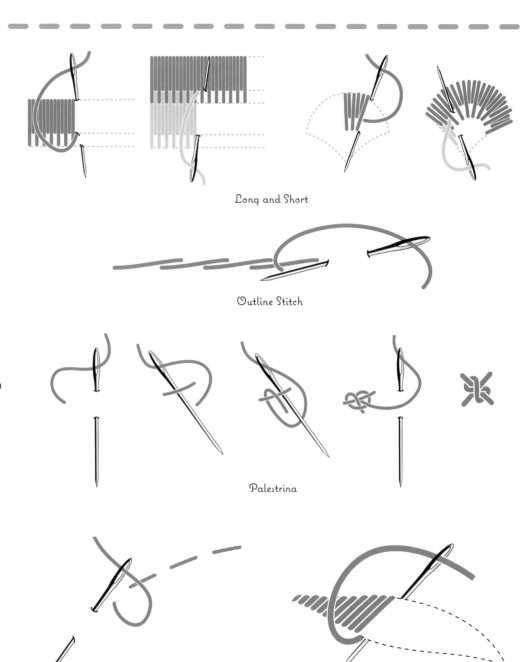

Long and Short

Outline Stitch

Palestrina

Running Stitch

Satin Stitch

Straight Stitch

Generally used as a single, individual stitch in any direction.

Whipped Backstitch

Stitch all backstitches. Then weave a whipping thread at one end over and under the backstitches without piercing the fabric.

Whipped Spider Stitch

A series of backstitches around a series of straight stitches, it resembles a wheel.

Whipped Stem Stitch

Complete evenly spaced Stem stitches. Then wrap it with a whipping thread without piercing the fabric.

Whipstitch

An overcast stitch often used to finish edges or join two fabrics together. Pull each whipstitch tight for a neat, finished appearance.

Straight Stitch

Whipped Backstitch

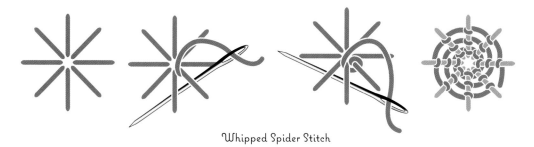

Whipped Spider Stitch

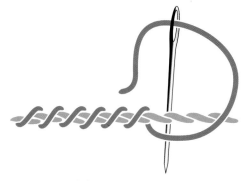

Whipped Stem Stitch

Whipstitch

Woven Picot

Make a loop on top of the fabric. Use a pin to hold the loop in place and weave the thread over and under the loop without piercing the fabric.

Slipstitch

A simple continuous stitch (not shown) used to close seams or attach items such as appliqués. Slip the needle through one fabric edge to anchor the thread, then take a small stitch through the fold or edge and pull the needle through. In the other edge or appliqué, insert the needle directly opposite the stitch you just made. Keep adding small stitches to connect the pieces.

Woven Picot

Project Templates

Belt of Many Paisleys, page 93

Enlarge to desired size

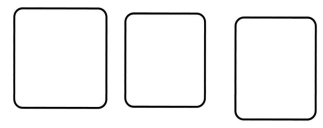

Festival Felt Scarf, page 106

Enlarge to desired size

Natural Setting, page 66

Enlarge to desired size

Sweet Treat Pincushion, page 81

Enlarge to desired size

Twirling Flower Coasters,
page 27

Enlarge to desired size

Summer's End Pillow, page 100

Enlarge to desired size

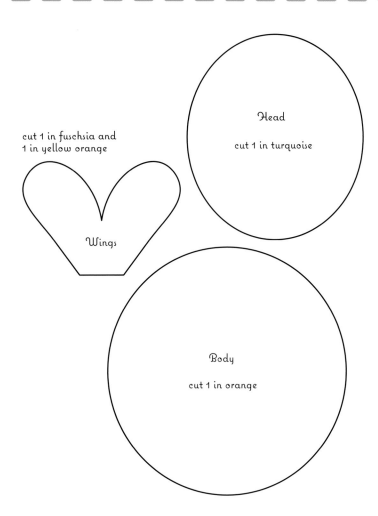

cut 1 in fuschia and
1 in yellow orange

Wings

Head

cut 1 in turquoise

Body

cut 1 in orange

Bee Colorful Pincushion,
page 97
Enlarge to desired size

Bright Rings Bookmark,
page 84
Enlarge to desired size

Night and Day Hobo Bag,
page 42

Enlarge to desired size

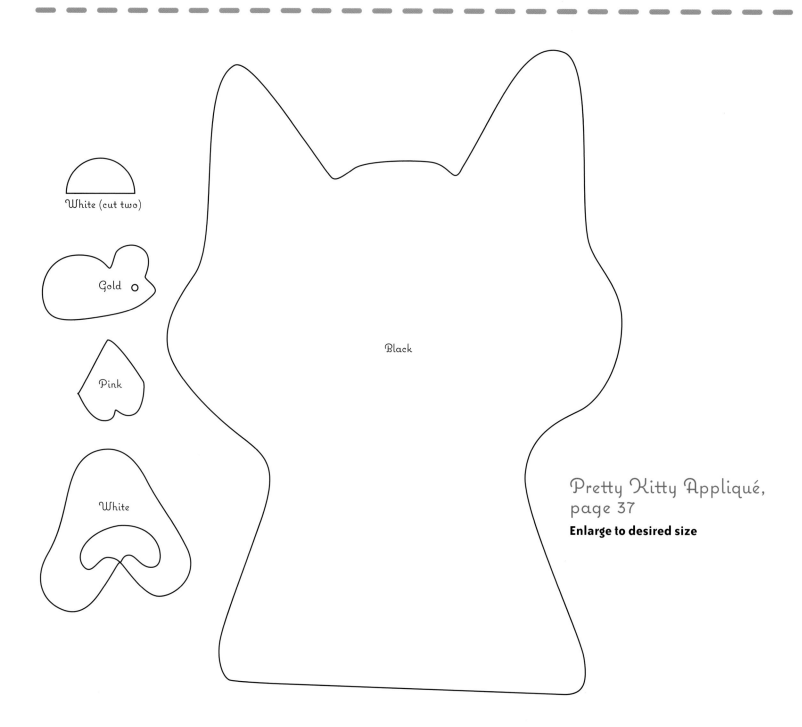

White (cut two)

Gold

Pink

White

Black

Pretty Kitty Appliqué, page 37

Enlarge to desired size

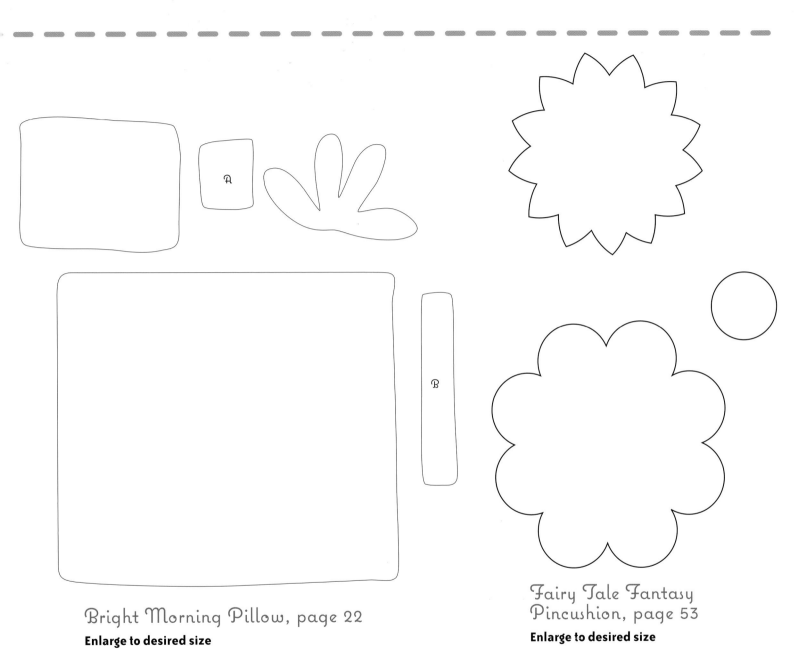

Bright Morning Pillow, page 22

Enlarge to desired size

Fairy Tale Fantasy
Pincushion, page 53

Enlarge to desired size

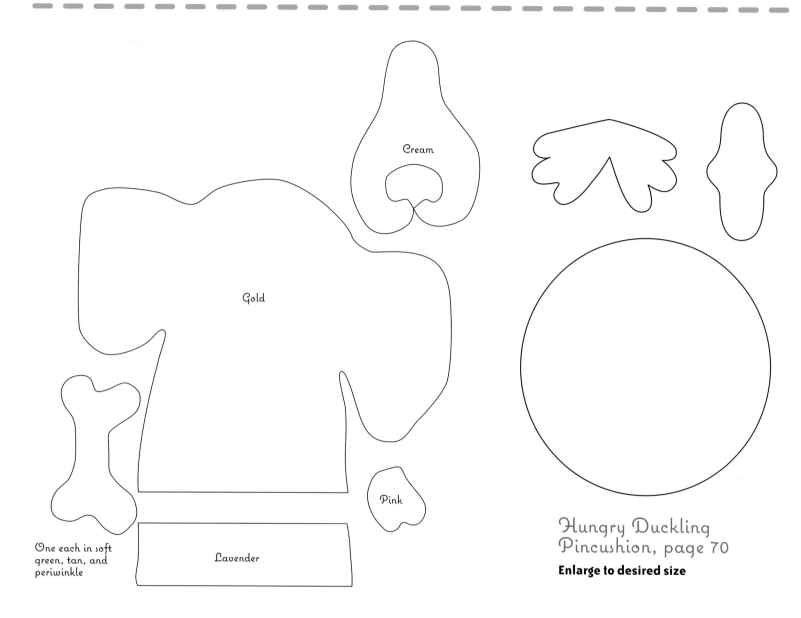

Cream

Gold

One each in soft green, tan, and periwinkle

Lavender

Pink

Fluffy Puppy Appliqué,
page 75
Enlarge to desired size

Hungry Duckling
Pincushion, page 70
Enlarge to desired size

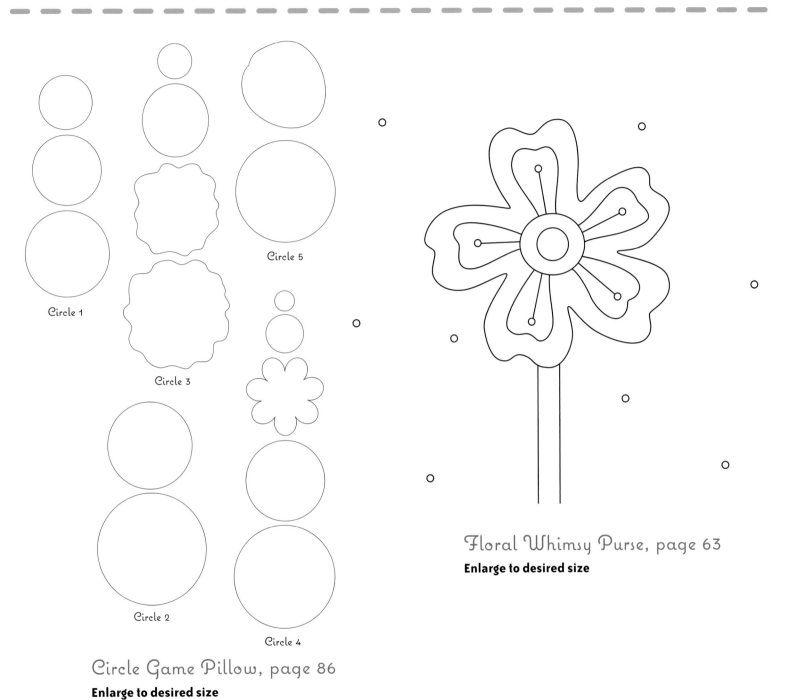

Circle 1

Circle 5

Circle 3

Circle 2

Circle 4

Circle Game Pillow, page 86

Enlarge to desired size

Floral Whimsy Purse, page 63

Enlarge to desired size

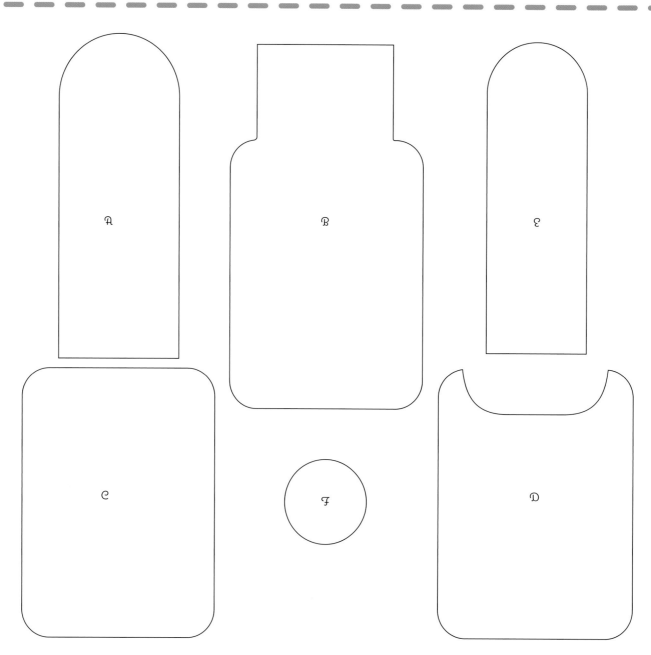

Desert Sky Phone Carrier, page 90

Enlarge to desired size

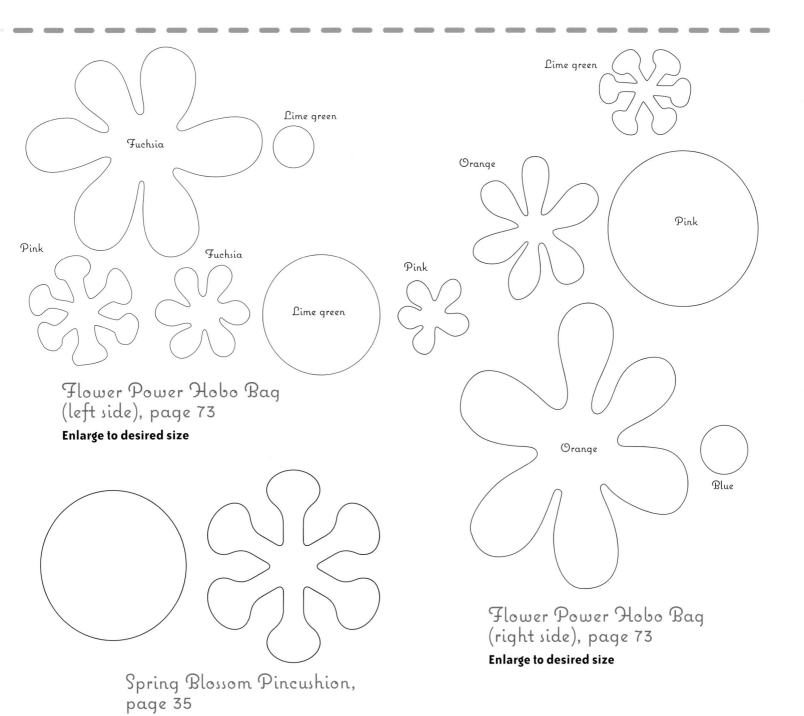

Lime green

Fuchsia

Lime green

Orange

Pink

Pink

Fuchsia

Pink

Lime green

Flower Power Hobo Bag
(left side), page 73

Enlarge to desired size

Orange

Blue

Flower Power Hobo Bag
(right side), page 73

Enlarge to desired size

Spring Blossom Pincushion,
page 35

Enlarge to desired size

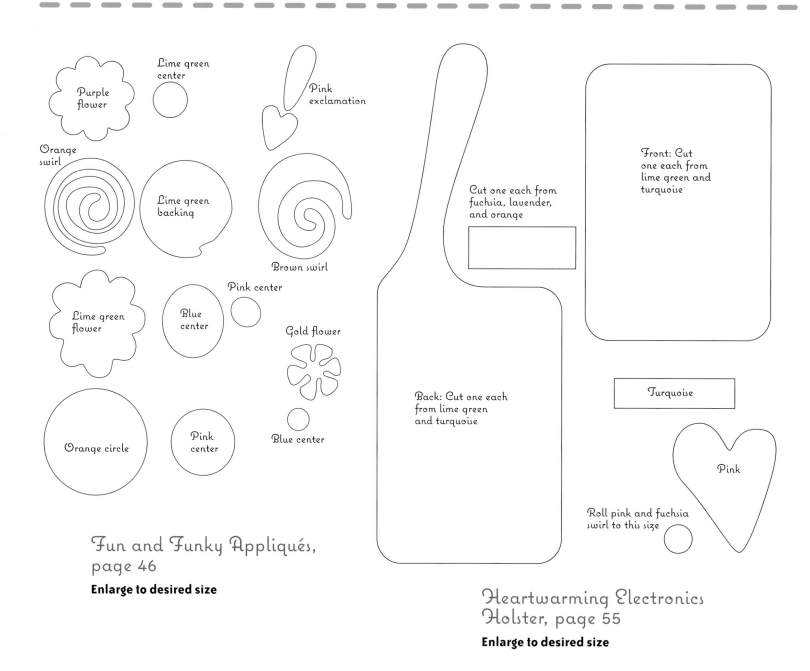

Purple flower

Lime green center

Pink exclamation

Front: Cut one each from lime green and turquoise

Orange swirl

Lime green backing

Brown swirl

Cut one each from fuchsia, lavender, and orange

Lime green flower

Blue center

Pink center

Gold flower

Blue center

Back: Cut one each from lime green and turquoise

Turquoise

Orange circle

Pink center

Pink

Roll pink and fuchsia swirl to this size

Fun and Funky Appliqués, page 46

Enlarge to desired size

Heartwarming Electronics Holster, page 55

Enlarge to desired size

May Flowers Purse, page 103
Enlarge to desired size

Book Buddy Blossom, page 44
Enlarge to desired size

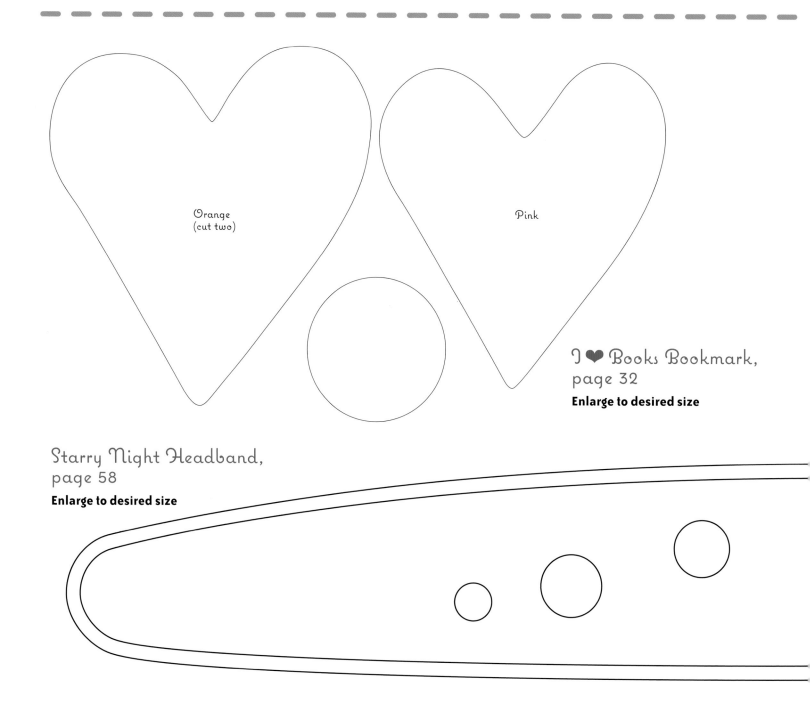

Orange
(cut two)

Pink

I ♥ Books Bookmark,
page 32
Enlarge to desired size

Starry Night Headband,
page 58
Enlarge to desired size

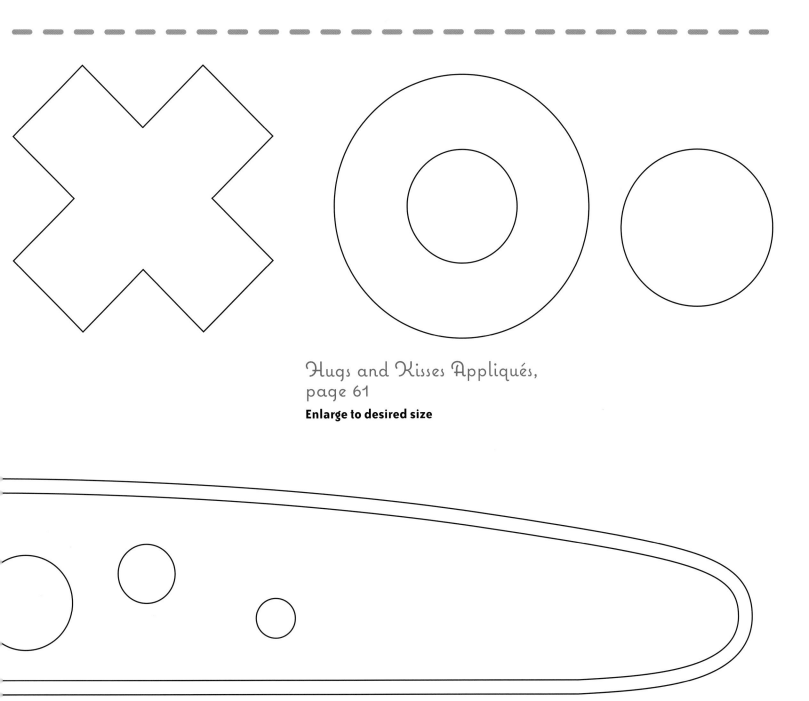

Hugs and Kisses Appliqués,
page 61

Enlarge to desired size

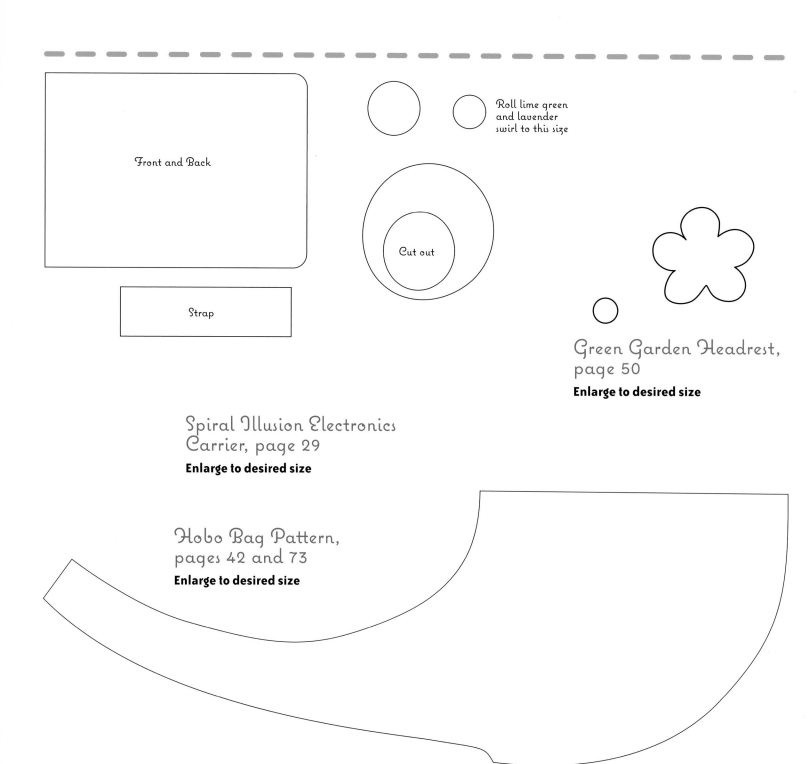

Front and Back

Strap

Roll lime green
and lavender
swirl to this size

Cut out

Green Garden Headrest,
page 50

Enlarge to desired size

Spiral Illusion Electronics
Carrier, page 29

Enlarge to desired size

Hobo Bag Pattern,
pages 42 and 73

Enlarge to desired size

About the Authors

Donna Kooler

Donna Kooler is cofounder, president, and creative director of Kooler Design Studio in Pleasant Hill, California. She says her job, above all, is to inspire her staff to "produce the highest-quality designs available in the marketplace." Under Donna's direction, Kooler Design Studio produces needlework, craft, knitting, crochet, quilting, and painting kits, leaflets, and books. The studio and its designers have won numerous awards, including the Outstanding Award of Excellence from P.J.S. Publishing, the Golden Needle Award, and numerous Charted Designer of America Awards.

Linda Gillum

Award-winning designer and fine artist Linda Gillum is cofounder and executive vice president of Kooler Design Studio. Her diverse design skills are expressed in all the needlework disciplines. Linda's artistic background is in watercolors, oil paintings, and pastel drawings, but she is always creating something new and different. Although she is well known for her coordinated baby ensembles and teddy bears, her affection is for animals, expressed in her paintings of dogs—sometimes with their owners! This book of embroidered felt projects is a showcase for Linda's love of needlework. She has a degree in business from St. Mary's College of California in Moraga, California, and a degree in art from the California College of the Arts in Oakland, California.

Acknowledgments

We wish to acknowledge the indispensable help and support we received from Priscilla Timm. We have counted on her advice and dedication for more than 25 years, and working on this book was no different. We also wish to thank Virginia Hanley-Rivett and Char Randolph, who stitched the beautiful projects and proofed the instructions. We give high praise to our entire dedicated staff, who work together every day, year after year, to ensure that each and every book, design, and project is the best it can be.

— Donna Kooler and Linda Gillum

Working with Donna Kooler, Linda Gillum, and the Kooler Design Studio team has been a creative pleasure. The Lark Books staff also showed its commitment to excellence in these pages. Beth Sweet, Larry Shea, Mark Bloom, Rosemary Kast, Beth Baumgartel, and Elizabeth Degenhard formed a fine editorial team. Art director Stacey Budge's terrific design complements the fun, colorful embroidered felt projects. Stacey was ably supported in art production by Bradley Norris. Thanks also go to Bernie Wolf and Orrin Lundgren, whose talents are illustrated by their artwork in this book, and to Susan McBride, for her playful cover design.

— Ray Hemachandra, Senior Editor

Index

It's all on www.larkbooks.com

Can't find the materials you
need to create a project?
Search our database for craft suppliers
& sources for hard-to-find materials.

Got an idea for a book?
Read our book proposal
guidelines and contact us.

Want to show off your work?
Browse current calls for entries.

Want to know what new and
exciting books we're working on?
Sign up for our free e-newsletter.

Feeling crafty?
Find free, downloadable
project directions on the site.

Interested in learning more about
the authors, designers & editors
who create Lark books?